WY PLAY HOUSE

Jerusalem

by **Simon Armitage**

Director	**John Tiffany**
Designer	**Laura Hopkins**
Composer/Arranger	**John Harris**
Lighting Designer	**Natasha Chivers**
Sound Designer	**Mic Pool**
Associate Director (Movement)	**Steven Hoggett**
Casting Director	**Kay Magson**
DSM	**Jonathan Ennis**

First performance at West Yorkshire Playhouse,
Courtyard Theatre, Leeds on 12 November 2005

D1646240

The Company

Narrator	**Joseph Alessi**
Spoon	**George Layton**
John Edward Castle	**Geoff Leesley**
Rose Castle	**Brigit Forsyth**
Wesley Castle	**Lee Warburton**
Wagstaff	**Simeon Truby**
Gert Castle/Sarah	**Ruth Alexander-Rubin**

Signed Performance
Tuesday 22 November 7.45pm
Interpreted by Ann Marie Bracchi

Captioned Performance
Wednesday 30 November 7.45pm

Audio Described performances
Saturday 26 November 2.30pm
Thursday 1 December 7.45pm
Audio described by Maggie Mash & Lynn Ecroyd

Please note that smoking or the use of cameras or recording equipment
is not permitted. Please ensure that mobile phones, pagers and digital
alarms are SWITCHED OFF before you enter the auditorium.

CAST

Joseph Alessi
Narrator

Theatre credits include: *The Postman Always Rings Twice* (West End/West Yorkshire Playhouse); *The Io Passion* (Aldeburgh/Almeida); *The Play What I Wrote* (Tour); *A Midsummer Night's Dream* (Regent's Park Open Air Theatre); *The Front Page, The Accrington Pals, Tovarich, Henry VIII, Arsenic and Old Lace* (Chichester Festival Theatre); *Polygraph* (Nottingham Playhouse); *The Taming of the Shrew* (Royal Exchange Theatre); *Light* (Theatre de Complicite); *The Rivals* (Haymarket, Basingstoke/Greenwich); *Animal Crackers* for which he was nominated for an Olivier award for Best Supporting Actor in a Musical (Royal Exchange/West End); *The Colour Of Justice* (Tricycle Theatre); *Jackie – An American Life, Laughter on the 23rd Floor* (Queens Theatre/West End); *Much Ado About Nothing, View from a Bridge, Romeo and Juliet* (Royal Exchange Theatre); *The Taming of the Shrew* (Leicester Haymarket); *The Snow Queen* (West Yorkshire Playhouse); *The Comedy of Errors* (RSC); *Hiawatha* (Cleveland Theatre Company).

Television credits include: *Revelations, Holby City, In a Land of Plenty, History Files, Wing and a Prayer, Kavanagh QC, Spywatch, Pie in the Sky, 99-1, The Chief, Minder, All in the Game.*

Film credits include: *The Other Woman, Family Business, Bridget Jones' Diary, London Kills Me, The Institute Benjamenta, Chaplin.*

Ruth Alexander-Rubin
Gert Castle/Sarah

Theatre credits include: *Sweet William, Comedy of Errors* (Northern Broadsides); *Company* (Ipswich New Wolsey Theatre); *Blonde Bombshells* (West Yorkshire Playhouse); *From a Jack to a King* (Oldham Coliseum); *Rasputin* (National tour); *Return to the Forbidden Planet* (Bolton Octagon Theatre); *Les Miserables* (UK Tour & Dublin); *A Funny Thing Happened on the Way to the Forum, Hard Times, Jack and the Beanstalk* (Hornchurch Queens Theatre); *Much Ado About Nothing* (Ludlow Festival); *A Midsummer Night's Dream* (English Theatre, Vienna); *Cabaret* (Lancaster Duke's Theatre); *Too Much Too Young, Dick Whittington* (London Bubble); *Treasure Island, Alice in Boogie Wonderland, Puss in Blue Suede Boots* (Liverpool Everyman).

Radio credits include: *Gertrud* (BBC).

Brigit Forsyth
Rose Castle

Theatre credits include: *Arsenic & Old Lace*, *Humble Boy* (National tour); *High Society* (Regent's Park Open Air Theatre); *Hamlet*, *Single Spies* (West Yorkshire Playhouse); *All My Sons*, *Amy's View*, *The Price*, *Tom and Viv* (Manchester Library Theatre); *The Cello and the Nightingale* (York Theatre Royal); *Morning Glory* (Watford Palace Theatre); *The Importance of Being Earnest*, *Little Murders*, *The Comedy of Errors* (Manchester Royal Exchange); *The Glass Menagerie* (Theatr Clwyd); *The Norman Conquests* (The Globe and Apollo Theatre, London); *Dusa, Stas, Fish and Vi* (Hampstead and Mayfair Theatres, London); *The Maintenance Man*, *You Must Be My Husband*, *My Fat Friend* (National tours).

Television credits include: *Whatever Happened to the Likely Lads*, *Emmerdale*, *Survival*, *Playing the Field*, *Tom, Dick and Harriet*, *The Practise*, *Sharon and Elsie*, *Down To Earth*, *The Eustace Bros.*, *Nice Town*, *Dangerfield*, *Spark*, *Bazaar and Rummage*, *Murder Most Horrid*, *Casualty*, *The Dark Season*, *The Master of Ballantree*, *The Bill*, *Wycliffe*, *The Ward*, *The Sinners*, *Adam Smith*, *Running Wild*, *Poirot*, *Boon*.

Film credits include: *Whatever Happened to the Likely Lads*, *Stanley's Vision*, *Fanny and Elvis*.

Brigit has worked extensively in radio.

George Layton
Spoon

Theatre credits include: *Chicago* (Adelphi Theatre); *Oliver!* (London Palladium); *More Lies About Jerzy* (New End Theatre, London); *Comedians* (Oxford Stage Company); *Bedroom Farce* (Theatre Royal Windsor); *Billy Liar*, *Of Blessed Memory* (King's Head Theatre, London); *Chapter Two* (Lyric Theatre, Hammersmith); *Chips with Everything* (Royal Court/New York); *Funny Peculiar* (Theatre Royal Sydney/Comedy Theatre Melbourne); *How to Succeed in Business Without Really Trying* (Churchill Theatre, Bromley); *Donkeys Years* (UK tour); *Twelfth Night* (Belgrade Theatre, Coventry); *Sir Thomas More* (Nottingham Playhouse).

Television credits include: *E=mc²*, *Sunburn*, *Holby City*, *Doctor in the House*, *Doctor at Large*, *Doctor in Charge*, *It Ain't Half Hot Mum*, *Minder*, *Robin's Nest*, *The Sweeney*, *The Likely Lads*, *Metropolis*.

Film credits include: *Don't Go Breaking My Heart*, *Here We Go Round the Mulberry Bush*, *Mosquito Squadron*.

Radio credits include: *Do Nothing Till You Hear From Me, Giles Webly Hogg Goes Into..., Quote, Unquote.*

Television writing credits include: *Don't Wait Up* (which won a Television and Radio Industries Club Best Comedy Award), *Executive Stress, Doctor in the House, Robins Nest.* Film writing credits include: *Boocock, the Pigeon and Me.*

Books: *The Fib and Other Stories, The Swap and Other Stories, The Trick and Other Stories* (to be published in 2006).

Geoff Leesley
John Edward Castle

Theatre credits include: *The Knight of the Burning Pestle* (Young Vic/ Colchester); *The Seagull* (Colchester Mercury); *Making Waves* (Stephen Joseph); *Merry Wives of Windsor, King John, The Cracked Pot* (Northern Broadsides); *Road* (Royal Exchange); *Albert Finney Doesn't Live Here Any More* (Library Theatre); *The Provoked Wife, Bedroom Farce* (National Theatre); *The Power of Darkness, Scraps, Largo Desolato* (Orange Tree Theatre); *Hobson's Choice, Oh Fair Jerusalem* (Birmingham Rep).

Television credits include: *Little Britain, Doctors, Coronation Street, EastEnders, Holby City, In Search of the Brontes, Walking on the Moon, A Life for a Life, Casualty, Brookside, Bergerac.*

Film credits include: *Wimbledon, Ashes & Sand, Asylum, Wilde, Second Best, The Frontline, Black Carrion.*

Radio credits include: many plays for BBC Radio and Capital Radio.

Simeon Truby
Wagstaff

Theatre credits include: *The Red Balloon* (Royal National Theatre); *The Duchess of Malfi, Rutherford and Son* (Salisbury Playhouse); *Chess, Blood Brothers, Hold Tight It's 60's Night* (National tours); *Antony and Cleopatra, As You Like It, Bring Me Sunshine* (Manchester Royal Exchange); *Schweyk in the Second World War* (Manchester Library); *Love's Labours Lost, Henry VIII, Taming of the Shrew* (Mappi Mundi); *Pinocchio* (Birmingham Rep); *The Hired Man, Romeo and Juliet, The Wizard of Oz, The Snow Queen, A Christmas Carol, Cinderella, Charley's Aunt, The Lakers* (Keswick Theatre by the Lake); *A Midsummer Night's Dream, Kes, Eight Miles High* (Bolton Octagon); *Macbeth* (Demi-Paradise).

Television credits include: *Island at War, A Touch of Frost, Coronation Street, The Royal.*

Lee Warburton
Wesley Castle

Theatre credits include: *Passport to Pimlico* (National tour); *The Holly and the Ivy* (National tour); *Romeo and Juliet* (Stafford Gatehouse); *The Soldier's Tale* (Music Theatre Wales).

Television credits include: *Heartbeat, MIT, Casualty, Bob and Rose, Where The Heart Is, Hope and Glory, Clocking Off, Queer as Folk, Wing and a Prayer, Coronation Street, Family Affairs.*

Film credits include: *Dogtribe.*

CREATIVES

Simon Armitage
Writer

Simon Armitage was born in 1963 and lives in West Yorkshire.

He has published nine volumes of poetry including *Killing Time*, 1999 (Faber & Faber) and *Selected Poems*, 2001 (Faber & Faber). His most recent collections are *The Universal Home Doctor* and *Travelling Songs*, both published by Faber & Faber in 2002. He has received numerous awards for his poetry including the Sunday Times Author of the Year, one of the first Forward Prizes and a Lannan Award.

He writes for radio, television and film, and is the author of four stage plays, including *Mister Heracles*, a version of Euripides' *The Madness of Heracles*. His recent dramatisation of *The Odyssey*, commissioned by the BBC, was broadcast on Radio 4 in 2004 and won a 2005 Spoken Word Award. He received an Ivor Novello Award for his song-lyrics in the Channel 4 film *Feltham Sings*, which also won a BAFTA.

His first novel, *Little Green Man*, was published by Penguin in 2001. His second novel *The White Stuff* was published in 2004.

Simon Armitage has taught at the University of Leeds and the University of Iowa's Writers' Workshop, and currently teaches at Manchester Metropolitan University. With Robert Crawford he edited *The Penguin Anthology of Poetry from Britain and Ireland since 1945*. Other anthologies include *Short and Sweet – 101 Very Short Poems*, and a selection of Ted Hughes' poetry, both published by Faber & Faber.

The Shout, a book of new and selected poems was published in the US in April 2005 by Harcourt. He is currently working on a translation of the middle English classic poem *Sir Gawain and the Green Knight*, commissioned by Faber & Faber in the UK and Norton in the US.

John Tiffany
Director

John was born in Huddersfield and trained at Glasgow University. He has recently been appointed Associate Director (New Work) at the National Theatre of Scotland. Before that he was Associate Director at Paines Plough and Literary Director at the Traverse.

Theatre credits include: *Playhouse Creatures* (West Yorkshire Playhouse); *Las Chicas del Tres y Media Floppies* (Granero Theatre, Mexico City/Edinburgh Festival); *If Destroyed True*, *Mercury Fur*, *The Straits* (Paines Plough); *Gagarin Way* (Traverse/RNT/Arts Theatre/world tour); *Among Unbroken Hearts* (Traverse/Bush Theatre); *Abandonment* (Traverse); *Perfect Days* (Traverse/Hampstead/Vaudeville/tour); *Passing Places* (Traverse/Citizens/ tour).

Laura Hopkins
Designer

Theatre credits include: *Mister Heracles* (TMA award for Best Design), *Dealers Choice*, *Kes*, *Betrayal* (West Yorkshire Playhouse); *The Storm*, *Dido, Queen of Carthage*, *The Golden Ass*, *Macbeth* (Shakespeare's Globe); *Le Comte Ory* (Garsington Opera); *Faustus*, *Othello* (both nominated for TMA awards), *Hamlet* (Northampton Royal); *Mercury Fur* (Paines Plough); *The INS Broadcasting Unit* (ICA); *Elixir of Love* (New Zealand Opera); *Carnesky's Ghost Train* (Old Truman Brewery, London); *Cosi Fan Tutte* (English National Opera); *Falstaff* (ENO/Opera North).

Laura has collaborated on numerous devised pieces including: *Clair de Luz* and *Hotel Methuselah* (Imitating the Dog).

John Harris
Composer/Arranger

Theatre credits include: *East Coast Chicken Supper*, *The Nest*, *Family*, *Kill The Old Torture Their Young*, *Perfect Days*, *Greta*, *Knives in Hens*, *Anna Weiss*, *Sharp Shorts* (Traverse Theatre); *Solstice*, *Midwinter* (RSC); *Il Bellissimo Silencio*, *Of Nettles and Roses*, *Stockaree* (Theatre Workshop); *Drummers* (Out of Joint).

Film and television credits include: *Paternoster*, *The Emperor*, *The Green Man of Knowledge*.

John is director of the award-winning experimental internet music company Seven Things, and artistic director of the News Arts Ensemble. He also performs and writes with his multi-instrumental group SPKE. He was organist of St Giles' Cathedral Edinburgh from 1997-2000.

Natasha Chivers
Lighting Designer

Theatre credits include: *My Mother Said I Never Should, Playhouse Creatures* (West Yorkshire Playhouse); *Horror For Wimps, Very Little Women* (Lipservice Theatre Company); *Renaissance* (Greenwich and Docklands International Festival); *Dirty Wonderland* (Frantic Assembly/Brighton Festival); *Who's Afraid Of Virginia Woolf?, Ma Rainey's Black Bottom, The Entertainer* (Liverpool Playhouse); *Hymns* (Frantic Assembly/Lyric Hammersmith); The Paines Plough Season at The Chocolate Factory including *Mercury Fur* (Plymouth Drum), *Small Things, Pyrenees* (The Tron Theatre Glasgow), *If Destroyed Still True* (Dundee Rep); Liverpool Everyman 40th Anniversary Season including *Urban Legend* and *The Kindness Of Strangers; Unexpected Man, Present Laughter* (Bath Theatre Royal); *Who's Afraid Of The Big Bad Book* (Soho Theatre); *The Straits* (59 East 59, New York/Paines Plough/Hampstead Theatre); *Memory Of Water* (Watford Palace Theatre); *The Bomb-itty of Errors* (New Ambassadors); *The Cherry Orchard, After The Dance* (Oxford Stage Company); *Peepshow* (Frantic Assembly/Plymouth Theatre Royal/Lyric Hammersmith/Tour); *On Blindness* (Paines Plough/Frantic Assembly/Graeae); *The Drowned World* (Paines Plough/Traverse Theatre/Bush Theatre); *Tiny Dynamite* (Frantic Assembly/Paines Plough/Lyric Hammersmith/International tour).

Mic Pool
Sound Designer

In a twenty-eight year career in theatre sound, Mic has been resident at the Lyric Theatre Hammersmith, the Royal Court Theatre, Tyne Theatre Company and toured internationally with Ballet Rambert. He has designed the sound for over 300 productions including more than 170 for the West Yorkshire Playhouse where he is currently Director of Creative Technology. He received a TMA award in 1992 for Best Designer (Sound) for *Life Is A Dream* and was nominated for both the Lucille Lortel and the Drama Desk Award for Outstanding Sound Design 2001 for the New York production of *The Unexpected Man.*

Recent theatre credits include: *The Postman Always Rings Twice* (Playhouse Theatre); *Ying Tong* (New Ambassadors Theatre); *The Solid Gold Cadillac* (Garrick Theatre); *Brand* (RSC/West End); *Pretending To Be Me* (West Yorkshire Playhouse/West End); *Art* (West End/Broadway/worldwide); *Shockheaded Peter* (Cultural Industry world tour/West End);

The Unexpected Man (RSC/West End/Broadway/Los Angeles); *Another Country* (Arts Theatre); *Beauty and the Beast, A Midsummer Night's Dream, The Seagull, Victoria, Romeo and Juliet, Twelfth Night, The Roundhouse Season of Late Shakespeare Plays* (RSC); *Three Thousand Troubled Threads* (Stelar Quines, EIF); *Blues in the Night, A Doll's House, David Copperfield, The 39 Steps, Twelfth Night, My Mother Said I Never Should* (West Yorkshire Playhouse); *Homage to Catalonia* (West Yorkshire Playhouse/Northern Stage/Teatre Romea).

Video work for theatre includes: *The Solid Gold Cadillac* (West End); *Dracula* (The Touring Consortium); *The Lion, the Witch and the Wardrobe, The Wizard of Oz, Johnson Over Jordan, Crap Dad* (West Yorkshire Playhouse); *Dangerous Corner* (West Yorkshire Playhouse/West End); *Singin' In The Rain* (West Yorkshire Playhouse/Royal National Theatre/ national tour); *The Turk In Italy* (ENO); *The Ring Cycle* (New National Theatre Tokyo); *Il Tabarro, Chorus!* (WNO); *Das Rheingold, Die Walküre* (Royal Opera House).

Television includes the sound design for *How Wide is Your Sky* (Real Life Productions for Channel Four); *Lesley Garrett and Friends at the Movies* (BBC).

Steven Hoggett
Associate Director (Movement)

Steven is co-founder and Artistic Director with Frantic Assembly.

Director/performer credits for Frantic Assembly include: *Hymns, On Blindness* (co-production with Paines Plough and Graeae); *Tiny Dynamite* (co-production with Paines Plough); *Heavenly, Sell Out, Zero, Flesh, Klub, Look Back In Anger.*

Directorial credits include: *Dirty Wonderland, Rabbit, Peepshow, Underworld* (Frantic Assembly); *Service Charge* (Lyric Hammersmith); *Air* (MAC, Birmingham).

Choreography and movement direction credits include: *Mercury Fur, The Straights* (Paines Plough); *Vs* (Karim Tonsi Dance Company, Cairo); *Waving* (Oily Carte); *Improper* (Bare Bones Dance Company); *Subterrain* (Farm Productions).

Additional performance credits include: *Manifesto* (Volcano Theatre Company); *Go Las Vegas* (The Featherstonehaughs); *Outside Now* for Prada (Milan Fashion Week 2001).

Kay Magson CDG
Casting Director

For the West Yorkshire Playhouse shows include: *My Mother Said I Never Should*, *Twelfth Night*, *A Doll's House*, *Singin' In The Rain* (and tour), *Martin Guerre* (and tour), *Bat Boy* (and West End), *Hamlet*, *McKellen Ensemble Season*, *Blues In The Night*, *The Madness of George III* (with Birmingham Rep), *Popcorn* (original production with Nottingham Playhouse), *The Beatification of Area Boy*, *Enjoy*, *A Small Family Business*, *Johnson Over Jordan*, *Eden End*, *Macbeth*, *The Taming of the Shrew*, *Mister Heracles*, *Kes*, *Electricity*, *Wind in the Willows*, *The Accrington Pals* and many others.

Other theatre credits include: *Assassins* (Sheffield Theatres); *The Solid Gold Cadillac* (Garrick); *Round The Horne... Revisited* (National Tour); *Dracula* (Bromley/National Tour); *Alfie: The Musical*, *Queen's English*, *The Country Wife*, *Mother Goose*, *Cinderella* (Watford); *Ma Rainey's Black Bottom*, *Still Life*, *The Astonished Heart*, *Dr Faustus*, *The Odd Couple*, *Who's Afraid Of Virginia Woolf?*, *Chimps*, *The Tempest* (Liverpool Everyman Playhouse); *Saved* (Bolton Octagon); *Old King Cole* (Unicorn); *Brassed Off* (Liverpool Playhouse/Birmingham Rep); *East Is East* (Pilot/York Theatre Royal/Octagon Bolton); *Macbeth* (Derby Playhouse).

Kay is a member of the Casting Directors' Guild.

WYPLAY HOUSE

West Yorkshire Playhouse

Since opening in 1990, West Yorkshire Playhouse has established a reputation both nationally and internationally as one of Britain's most exciting and active producing theatres, winning awards for everything from its productions to its customer service. The Playhouse provides both a thriving focal point for the communities of West Yorkshire and theatre of the highest standard for audiences throughout the region and beyond.

The Playhouse regularly collaborates with other venues and companies, sharing resources practically, financially and artistically to create exciting and spectacular performances. Recent work has included a tour of our production of **The 39 Steps** with Fiery Angel Ltd, Teatre Romea and Northern Stage for **Homage to Catalonia** – a production that premiered at the Playhouse then visited Paris, Newcastle and Barcelona and Kneehigh Theatre for **The Bacchae**, a co-production that subsequently toured nationally. Successful transfers include **Ying Tong**, which transferred to the New Ambassadors in association with Michael Codron, and **The Postman Always Rings Twice**, which transferred to the Playhouse Theatre with Ambassador Theatre Group. Following our successful partnership with Birmingham Rep in 2004 for **Madness of George III** and **A View From the Bridge** we're delighted to be working with them again for our Christmas production in 2006. Next year we also plan some exciting co-productions with Liverpool Theatres and Northern Broadsides.

Box Office: 0113 213 7700
www.wyp.org.uk

Housekeeping
Mary Ambrose, Eddy Dube, Mike Hilton, Ricky Spurr, Kevin Westwood and Sarah Wonnacott Cleaners*
Paul Robinson Dayman

I.T. Department
Ben Tinker I.T. Manager

Maintenance
Frank Monaghan Maintenance Manager
Tony Proudfoot and Mike Wallace* Maintenance Assistants

Marketing and Sales
Nick Boaden Marketing Manager
Angela Robertson Sales Development Manager
Joanna Down Marketing Officer
Kate Evans Marketing Officer
Bobby Brook Ambassadors Co-ordinator*
Aimee Green Graphic Design Officer
Caroline Laurent Box Office Manager
Bronia Daniels, Lynn Hudson, Mel Worman and David Salkeld Duty Supervisors
Rachael Fowler, Rebecca Gibson, Maureen Kershaw, Amy Mackay, Dena Marsh, Sarah McIver, Rosalind McKever, Charlie Sharman, Holly Thomas and Sam Ward Box Office Assistants

New Writing
Alex Chisholm Literary and Events Manager
Chris Thorpe BBC Writer In Residence
Jodie Marshall Writer on Attachment

Paint Shop
Virginia Whiteley Head Scenic Artist
Sarah East Freelance Scenic Artist

Performance Staff
Andy Charlesworth and Jon Murray Firemen
Andrew Ashdown, Beccy Ashdown, Daisy Babbington, Kathryn Beale, Rachel Blackerby, Andrew Bramma, Jennifer Bramma, Sangeeta Chana, Megan Christie, Jez Coram, Sarah Cullen, William Dawson, Leigh Exley, Shaun Exley, Amy Fawdington, Asha France, Averil Frederick, Rachael Frederick, Sophie Goodeve, Alison Goodison, Rory Girvan, Andrew Gilpin, Deb Hargreave, Becky Harding, Fiona Heseltine, Rachel Kendall, Claire Lindus, Robert Long, Victoria Long, Nathanya Laurent, Allan Mawson, Hayley Mort, Jo Murray, Soazig Nicholson, Monisha Roy, Pam Sandhu, Tim Sharry, Lucy Tallent, Holly Thomas, Helen West, Daneill Whyles and Rebekah Wilkes Attendants*

Press
Rachel Coles Head of Press
Leonie Osborne Acting Head of Press
Robert Farrell Assistant Press Officer

Production Electricians
Matt Young Chief Electrician
David Bennion-Pedley, Paul Halgarth and David Mitchell Electricians

Production Management
Suzi Cubbage Production Manager
Eddie de Pledge Production Manager
Dickon Harold Head of Technical Design
Christine Alcock Production Administrator

Props Department
Chris Cully Head of Props
Sarah Barry Props Supervisor
Susie Cockram and Scott Thompson Prop Makers
Lucy Adams Props Assistant

Restaurant and Bar
Charles Smith Food and Beverage Manager
Michael Montgomery Sous Chef
Louise Poulter Chef de Partie

Kirsty Crerar and Linda Monaghan Commis Chefs
Robert Cawood, Lee Moran and Robert Wright Kitchen Porters
Diane Kendall and Pauline Wilkes-Ruan Restaurant Supervisors
Lee Dennell, Jade Gough, Caron Hawley, Kath Langton* and Esther Lewis Restaurant Assistants
Alice Baxter, Rosanna Gordon, Scott Kennedy, Cheryl Lee, Harry Lee, Cati MacKenzie, Rachel Marriner, Julia Mudd, Jessica Rawlins, Sinead Rodgers, Hayley Smith, Hayley Tong, Justine Tong, William White and Jenny Yan Restaurant Assistants*
Graeme Thompson Bar Supervisor
Terence Whitlam and Graeme Randall Assistant Bar Supervisors*
Elizabeth Carter, Alice Ellerby, Dean Firth, Ruth Godfrey, Vicky Hemsley, Tracey Hodgetts, Lewis Smith and Karlene Wray Bar Assistants*
Gemma Schoffield Coffee Shop Assistant

Security
Denis Bray Security Manager
Frank Kamara and Glenn Slowther Security Officers

Sound Department
Andy Meadows Head of Sound
Martin Pickersgill Deputy Head of Sound
Mathew Angove Assistant Sound Technician
Aidy Parker Freelance Sound Technician

Technical Stage Management
Martin S Ross Technical Stage Manager
Michael Cassidy Deputy Technical Stage Manager
Nidge Solly Stage Technician
David Berrell, Matt Hooban, Matt de Pledge and Sarah Platts Stage Crew

Theatre Operations
Jeni Douglas House Manager
Pavla Beier, Jonathan Dean, Stuart Simpson* and Sheila Howarth Duty Managers

Touring Company
Gary Simpson and Neal Wright
Marc Walton Crew

Wardrobe Department
Stephen Snell Head of Wardrobe
Victoria Marzetti Deputy Head of Wardrobe
Becky Graham Wardrobe Supervisor
Julie Ashworth Head Cutter
Nicole Martin Cutter
Alison Barrett Costume Prop Maker/Dyer
Victoria Harrison and Catherine Lowe Wardrobe Assistants
Anne-Marie Hewitt Costume Hire Manager
Kim Freeland Wig and Make-up Supervisor
Catherine Newton Wardrobe Maintenance/ Head Dresser
Nadine Davies and Elaine Graham Dressers*

*Denotes part-time

WEST YORKSHIRE PLAYHOUSE CORPORATE SUPPORTERS

WYPLAY HOUSE

Sponsors of the Arts Development Unit

Media Sponsors

 My Mother Said I Never Should

The Lion, the Witch and the Wardrobe

DIRECTORS CLUB

Executive Members

Director Members

Halifax plc   Incasso Debt Recovery   Provident Financial

Associate Members

YORKSHIRE POST

West Yorkshire Playhouse gratefully acknowledges support from

The Pearson Playwrights' Scheme sponsored by Pearson Plc

CHARITABLE TRUSTS

Audrey and Stanley Burton 1960 Trust
Kenneth Hargreaves Charitable Trust
Clothworkers' Foundation
The Ragdoll Foundation

Harewood Charitable Settlement
The Frances Muers Trust
The Charles Brotherton Trust
Harold Hyam Wingate Foundation

If you would like to learn how your organisation can become involved with the success of
the West Yorkshire Playhouse please contact the Development Department on 0113 213 7275.

Simon Armitage
Jerusalem

ff
faber and faber

First published in 2005
by Faber and Faber Limited
3 Queen Square London WC1N 3AU

Typeset by Country Setting, Kingsdown, Kent CT14 8ES
Printed in England by Mackays of Chatham plc, Chatham, Kent

A CIP record for this book
is available from the British Library

ISBN 0-571-21666-8

2 4 6 8 10 9 7 5 3 1

Author's Note

A recent study of human behaviour concluded that any man left on his own with a tea-cosy will eventually put it on his head. Extending this logic to the setting of a northern social club, it could be imagined that anyone left alone with a shimmer-curtain, a microphone and a piano will eventually sing a song. The song of their dreams, possibly. In the first production of *Jerusalem* at West Yorkshire Playhouse, each of the main characters sang a classic or cult pop song at the most dramatic point of their story. In any subsequent production, it would be a matter for the directing team to decide where these 'tea-cosy moments' should occur in the play, and of which songs they should consist.

Characters

Narrator/Census Taker

John Edward Castle

Rose Castle

Wesley Castle

Gert Castle

Spoon

Wagstaff

*With a company of seven actors
all other roles can be doubled*

*'The Tide Rises, the Tide Falls',
the song which opens the play, is by
Henry Wadsworth Longfellow*

*The musical setting for the original production
was by Adam Carse*

JERUSALEM

Act One

Above Jerusalem. Dawn.

Song
> *The tide rises, the tide falls,*
> *the twilight darkens, the curlew calls.*
> *Along the sea-sands damp and brown*
> *the traveller hastens towards the town.*
> *And the tide rises, the tide falls.*

Narrator
> Early morning up on the heath.
> A finger-nail moon still hangs on its hook.
> The sky growing lighter out to the east –
> kindling smouldering under the hills.
> A mist in the hollows, like clouds asleep.

Song
> *Darkness settles on roofs and walls,*
> *but the sea, the sea in darkness calls.*
> *The little waves with their soft white hands*
> *efface the footprints in the sands.*
> *And the tide rises, the tide falls.*

Narrator
> A daffodil-yellow Transit van
> on a single road. It motors along,
> loses itself in a pillow of fog,
> then breaks the surface, bursts the air
> like a beast of the deep might suddenly fly
> from a silent, calm-as-a-millpond sea.
>
> All this so far from the coast.
> Spoon to his friends, Spoon to his face.

Somewhere beyond him the morning breaks.
The cat's-eyes stare, and so do the stars.

Song
The morning breaks, the steeds in their stalls
stamp and neigh as the hostler calls.
The day returns, but never more
returns the traveller to the shore.

Narrator
So the van comes to a stop. And Spoon
climbs out of the cab and stands on the edge,
looks down at the valley which starts at his feet:
Jerusalem town is coming to life, as the lights
in the street, like birthday candles, are snuffed out.

Spoon Thar she blows.

Song
And the tide rises, the tide falls.

Narrator
Jerusalem, where Father Noah spreads the news,
rehearses sermons from the pulpit
to an audience of empty pews.

Fr Noah As the vine trees among the trees of the forest,
which I have given to the fire for fuel, so will I give the
inhabitants of Jerusalem. Ezekiel, 15:6.

Narrator
In the attic room of a pig-sty squat
a New Age couple funnel musky liquid
into small bottles, out of a large vat.

Zak Pure essence, man. Neat.

Jade Psychic uplift in a flask, man. Karma on a stick.
Sweet.

Narrator
　　In the old mill,
　　a window writhes with shadows and light:
　　signs of life at this unearthly hour:
　　glamour photography on the second floor.

Cecil Lower. Lower. Let's try another with the lipstick
and the leopardskin, my flower.

Kylie Cecil, it's cold. It's like ice, your hand.

Cecil Goosebumps, like the flesh in bloom, my petal.
Now lie back and think of the promised land.

Narrator
　　There's the Fire Station next to the Town Hall,
　　with a telephone-hatch in a hole in the wall.

Hoax Caller I'd like to report a fire.

Duty Fireman Whereabouts?

Hoax Caller At the end of my cigarette. Ha ha ha.

Narrator
　　. . . well, split my sides and slap my thigh.
　　Meanwhile, in the corner of Spoon's horse-
　　　　chestnut eye
　　Jerusalem's shops are opening up for the day.

Spoon My God, the old place hasn't changed. Like it's
been kept under glass.

Narrator
　　There's Sugget & Sugget, Gentlemen's Outfitters,
　　up with the lark and out with the tape-measures.

Sugget 1 Might I suggest the pinstripe, sir, for business
purposes?

Sugget 2 One hundred per cent wool, sir, basically a
sheep with buttons and creases.

Narrator
> There's Boysie the butcher,
> reaching into a carcass for his petty cash.

Boysie Don't believe in banks. Keep it here, between the lungs and the heart.

Narrator
> There's Ellis Twistle, tobacconist,
> weighing out ready-rubbed in his collar and tie.

Twistle It's MCC. No gentleman should be unfastened at the neck, old bean.

Narrator
> And the Beardsley Brothers, mending a loose tile
> that cracked in the night, accidentally on purpose,
> no doubt.

Beardsley 1 Bigger job than we first thought. You're looking at three days' work and that's before we start.

Beardsley 2 Yeah, that's before we start.

Narrator
> And Jalopy Joe in his showroom, touching up
> some clapped-out rust-bucket with metallic paint,
> clamping the jump-leads onto a dead heart.

Jalopy Joe Come on, my beautiful, let's hear that spark of life.

Narrator
> And the Boots in the corner shop.
> Him and her. Hers and his.

Mrs Boot Jaffa Cake, your cod-liver oil capsule, and tea with two.

Mr Boot Thanking you.

Spoon Preserved in aspic, this place. The town where time stood still.

Song (*reprise*)
> *The tide rises, the tide falls.*
> *The twilight darkens, the curlew calls.*
> *Along the sea-sands damp and brown*
> *the traveller hastens towards the town.*

Narrator
> At 27 Lord Street, Spoon gets out, unlocks the van.
> It's a junk shop in there, a lifetime's collection of
> odds and sods.
>
> Across the road at 28 a curtain on the top floor
> twitches.
> John Edward Castle watches and watches,
> bites his lip till it bleeds and bleeds, and mutters . . .

JE Spoon. You bastard.

Narrator
> Downstairs, looking out from the parlour,
> Rose Castle's pulse pumps harder and harder,
> Rose Castle's heart beats faster and faster.

Song
> *And the tide rises, the tide falls.*

SCENE TWO

Outside Number 28. Census Taker knocks on door.
Wesley answers.

Census Taker Are you the occupier?

Wesley No, I'm his son.

Census Taker Could I speak with the occupier please,
if he's home?

Wesley Ah well, bit difficult, that. You see, he's
housebound, mi dad, got a room upstairs and doesn't
come down.

13

Census Taker It's the census, you see. If you could just tell me how many people live here – who they are, what they do and all the rest – won't take a minute.

Wesley Well, like I said, there's mi dad. John Edward Castle. He's fifty-eight, retired, er . . . pensioned off, you know, retired hurt, long-term sick sort of thing. He's on disability because of his legs and his back . . .

JE (*through Tannoy – a microphone-and-speaker arrangement on mantelpiece of front room, beneath portrait of John Edward in full fire-service uniform and medals*) Wesley, who's that? If it's the Jehovah's Witnesses tell 'em they can stick it where the spuds don't grow. Ey, what does a man have to do to get a cup of tea in this house? And will you mow that lawn today or we'll have to get a bloody combine harvester in. And get up the allotments and tell Ellis Twistle he's too late with them onions – I saw him putting 'em in yesterday, daft sod. And nip down the bookies with these bets, will you?

JE's bedroom.

JE (*into radio mic*) Testing, testing, one, two, three. You're listening to Radio Castle, the voice of Jerusalem. Now, before I go any further, I'd like to extend a warm welcome to Jerusalem's oldest exile, Mr Spoon, ex-policeman of this parish. To those who know him he won't need any introduction, and to those who don't, here's a bit of advice. Don't trust him as far as you could throw him, which won't be very far, looking at how much he's broadened with the years. And if you shake hands with him, count your fingers afterwards. OK, on with the show. I've got a few announcements to make. Firstly, a blue Burmese cat has gone missing from the vicinity of Alma Road. There's a five pound reward, please call me with any information. Secondly I've been sent a card asking me to say hello to a woman in Thorpe Close who's a hundred and eleven – oh, I'm sorry, I've misread that. Actually she's ill. Ha ha, ha. OK, listeners, it's phone-in time, and the lines are open. Anybody? I'm waiting.

On the doorstep.

Wesley So that's about it for mi dad.

Census Taker And is there a lady of the house?

Wesley Yes, mi mother, Rose. (*Shouts for her.*) Mum? She looks after mi dad, which is a full-time job in itself, but she's got this animal foodstuffs business which she runs out of the back yard – you know, pony nuts, maize, that kind of thing. (*She calls again.*) Mum? Mum?

Rose is on the phone, standing at the back door.

Rose (*to Wesley*) I'm on the phone. (*into phone*) So it's two bags of the cereal mix and three large tins of the meat. Sorry, three large bags of the cereal mix and two meat. It'll be Wednesday, or tomorrow if our Wesley's working the night-shift – he'll drop them round in the van. Now if I can just mention your account, it's five weeks now since . . . I know, but it would certainly help me if . . . I see, I see . . . Oh yes, a very valuable customer, Mr Armitage . . . yes, smallholdings, yes, yes . . . I'm sure that will be fine, whenever you're ready, there's no rush. Very good. Thanks again, then. Bye bye. (*Puts phone down.*) Tight as a camel's whatsit. In a sandstorm.

JE (*Tannoy*) Wesley, where's your mother? I wouldn't mind that sandwich now, and if I've got to have a sponge-down let's do it while the water's hot. And where's the bloody paper. Rose? Wesley? Rose. That sandwich, per – *lease.*

Doorstep.

Census Taker Which brings us to you.

Wesley Yeah. Look, tell me to shut up if I'm rabbiting on. I don't know how much you need to know.

Census Taker Oh, you're doing just fine, young man. You spill the beans, I'm writing it all down.

Wesley Well, I'm Wesley Castle, I'm twenty-four and I work for the Water Board. And I'm a volunteer in the local fire brigade – family business, you might say. I hate it.

Census Taker What is it you don't like – fires, or firemen?

Wesley Both.

Station Master (*voice from off*) What do you call that, young Castle? It's a good job we're not relying on it to put out any fire.

Fireman (*voice from off*) Come on everyone, last one up the pole's a lard-arse. Wesley, do the washing-up, love, there's a good chap. Plenty of *Fairy* – keep those hands nice and soft.

Wesley I'd rather be fishing. What else? Oh yeah, I'm doing psychology at night school, and I'm just reading Freud, so at some point I'm probably going to murder mi father and marry mi mother. Don't write that down. Er, I'm single but open to offers, and I wear glasses to read. That do you?

Census Taker Very thorough, young man. One final question: any pets?

Wesley No.

JE (*Tannoy*) Wesley, haven't you got rid of them yet? Bleeding God-botherers, poking their noses in . . .

Wesley Unless you include . . .

Census Taker Well, you've been most informative. Oh, by the way – can you tell me who lives over the road, at twenty-seven?

Wesley Feller called Spoon. Arrived last week. Seems to have settled in like he knows the place, but apart from that, I can't help you, mate.

Census Taker Not your job, young man, it's mine. The National Office of Statistics and Trends thanks you for your tellings and your time.

Wesley Pleasure.

Bleeper goes off.

Oh, Christ, got to run.

Narrator

So, our census taker crosses the road
but at twenty-seven there's nobody home.
Mr Spoon it seems is out and about,
getting a name for himself again,
getting the gist and the gen.
Not that there's much the people of town
don't know about him. Listen, the phones
are buzzing, tongues are wagging,
brains are racking, ears are wigging.
It's Sunday by now, so the bells are ringing.

Fr Noah And we welcome into our flock Mr Spoon, who was lost to us like the lamb far from the fold, who travelled amongst swooping eagles and ravenous wolves, but whose path lead him back to Jerusalem, his home, one of our own. Lord, with thy mercy –

Congregation Hear our prayer.

*

Zak So apparently this Spoon geezer was a big cheese in the fuzz right, had this town by the short-and-curlies. So there was him in the plod and that John Edward Castle dude doing the Pugh Pugh Barney McGrew number, and it was bad karma man, daggers drawn, ego central, top-dog-irresistible-force meets mother-of-all-immovable-objects, man, get my drift, yeah?

Jade Yeah. Cool.

*

Kylie And seemingly John Edward went into a burning barn on bonfire night to rescue a child, and down came a wooden beam – splat. And seemingly it was Spoon who dragged him out of the flames, and seemingly Spoon got a medal for bravery to the cause, and all John Edward got was paralysed from the Pennines down.

Cecil Language, Kylie, please.

Kylie So there's John Edward on life-support up the hospital, and seemingly Spoon goes to pay him a visit, and gets chatting with Rose in the cafeteria. Now, I'm not one for gossip, but rumour has it . . .

*

Sugget 1 So their eyes met over a mechanically-dispensed MaxPac coffee and a marshmallow snowball with coconut flakes.

Sugget 2 And that was it. Next news he was in here sprucing himself up. He wanted a suit like the Beatles wore – no cuffs, no lapels, no buttons. He said, how much is that?

Both We said, well . . . with all those extras.

*

Butcher And the way I heard it, she would have upped and offed, but was ill with the shame and the guilt. Now Mrs F, do you want that blood pudding wrapped, or in your hand for the way home?

*

Beardsley 1 Me and me bruv see it all from up here, don't we, our kid?

Beardsley 2 Don't miss a trick.

Beardsley 1 Anyhows, JE might have been flat on his back but he could still get the old man to rise to the occasion – know what I mean? Life in the old dog after all, lead in the pencil, because come Christmas his missus is in the pudding club . . .

Beardsley 2 . . . up the duff . . .

Beardsley 1 . . . eating for two, so it's happy families again, nappies on the line. And poor old Spoon, he goes sloping off . . .

Beardsley 2 . . . with his tail between his legs . . .

Beardsley 1 . . . gets wed to some Jackie, June, Jessica – and moves to Southport, Fleetwood, or Lytham, or some place over the hill . . .

Beardsley 2 . . . yeah, Lancashire. Tragic.

*

Twistle Ah yes. Janet. Janice? Janine? Nice woman, I heard. No Mona Lisa but kept herself tidy. Well, she died. And now he's back, our Mr Spoon. Stirring the old broth is the colloquial expression, I think you'll find.

*

In the corner shop.

Mrs Boot Is that *it*, Mr Spoon. Will that be *all*?

Spoon Yes, that's it. Oh, and one of those red roses, please, if they're fresh.

Mr Boot They're not.

Spoon Then I'll leave it. Thank you all the same.

Mrs Boot Thanking you, Mr Spoon.

Mr Boot Sir.

SCENE THREE

JE's bedroom. The phone rings.

JE Yes.

Wagstaff Alwin Wagstaff here, JE.

JE Alwin. How's the home entertainment business?

Wagstaff Oh, thriving, thriving. 'Wagstaff's Televisual Emporium, for all your viewing requirements at competitive prices.' By the way, have you thought about updating to NICAM stereo and a flat-screen, John Edward?

JE Yes, I've thought about it a lot. It's bollox.

Wagstaff Yes, you're probably right. Anyway, how are you?

JE Bad, if you must know. That creep Spoon's back in town, strolling around like a donkey with two dicks. What's his game? I thought I'd seen him off once. He's like a dog coming back to his own vomit, a fly sniffing around a pile of shi –

Wagstaff Well, quite, JE. But never mind him – I have news. As you know, I've been Entertainments Secretary at Jerusalem Social Club for ten years now. Ten distinguished years, even if I say so myself, and, well, to cut a long story short, it's time to stand down.

JE Oh, Alwin, that's wonderful news. Er, I mean it's wonderful that you've managed ten years, congratulations, but disappointing that you should be retiring, obviously.

Wagstaff Cut the candy-floss, I know you've been dying to jump in my grave. Now listen, I can't say the job's yours – there'll have to be a vote, and we've pencilled it in for November the fifth. But a man of your calibre should walk it, er, if you'll excuse the analogy.

JE Oh, Alwin . . .

Wagstaff Now look, we haven't had this phone call, alright? I've got to go, there's two-dozen DVD players due to fall off the back of a lorry at Five Lane Ends in half an hour, but can I take it you're happy to stand, er, I mean put yourself forward?

JE Oh Alwin, you can, my friend. You most certainly can. (*Puts phone down.*) Right, you fuckers, this is the big one. Twenty-odd years given up for dead – but I'll show 'em who's boss. I can see it now: intercom, telephone, Tannoy, close-circuit TV – I can run that club from right here. And Saturday night, live bingo with me on the big screen, calling the numbers, calling the shots. Kelly's eye – number one. Big Willie – ninety. Oh yes, things are going to change around here, you just watch. (*into Tannoy*) Rose, get me that Dixons catalogue and a glass of beer. (*to himself again*) Mobile phone, pager, web page – maybe I'll need one of those fancy tellies after all. I'll be right back in the thick of it, right back centre stage. (*Tannoy*) Rose, do you hear? Get up these stairs and listen to what I've got to say.

Downstairs. Spoon knocks on door of Number 28.

Spoon Rose, I didn't know whether to . . .

Rose Mr Spoon, is it drystuff you're after or tinned? We deliver on a Wednesday and there's ten per cent off for bulk orders. If you'd like a price list . . .

Spoon Come on, Rose. It's me. Say something. Something about us.

Rose You shouldn't have come here.

Spoon I've moved in over the road.

Rose So I see. Well, if it's a cup of sugar you're after, you can go to the shop on the corner.

Spoon I've been in there. They said if it was a Rose I wanted, I should try elsewhere. So here I am.

JE (*Tannoy*) Who's that at the door? It's like Piccadilly Circus, this place. Tell 'em to bugger off.

Spoon Still up there, is he?

Rose Still up there. Still going strong.

Spoon Look, Rose, let me just . . .

Rose No, let me. It was years ago. It's dead, right, so leave it. You went your way and I went mine. Now there's enough gossips in this street without me giving them something to blab about, so unless it's dog biscuits or a bale of straw you're after, I'll ask you to be on your way.

JE (*Tannoy*) Rose, who is it?

Rose (*shouting upwards*) It's nobody. Just somebody asking for directions.

JE (*Tannoy*) Who does he think we are, the bloody RAC? Tell him to buy a map.

Spoon You're right. That's what I thought you'd say, and you're right. But just tell me this. When you looked out of the window last week and saw me standing there in the street, didn't something stir?

JE (*Tannoy*) Oh, arseholes. Rose, will you come up and change this sheet?

Spoon Didn't some little electric shock run up and down your spine, didn't it tingle in you fingertips and toes, didn't it light up the ends of your hair? Rose?

Rose I think you've got me confused with one of those fibre-optic lamps you could buy in the seventies. There's no call for them around here. Goodbye, Mr Spoon.

The door closes

SCENE FOUR

Narrator
　　　　So the tide rises and the tide falls.
　　　　And high up in the blue-green hills
　　　　the cotton grass nods and the curlew calls.

　　　　Look down on Jerusalem's houses and mills:
　　　　where Jalopy Joe sells dodgy wheels,
　　　　where Father Noah heaps salmon spread
　　　　on wafers of communion bread,
　　　　where Zak and Jade bring to the boil
　　　　a vat-load of patchouli oil,
　　　　where Cecil's camera never lies,
　　　　and through the dark venetian blinds –
　　　　some glamour puss in zebra stripes
　　　　breaks cover when the flash-bulb strikes.
　　　　And where the Beardsley Brothers strut their stuff
　　　　like alley cats on hot tin roofs,
　　　　and Sugget takes an inside leg

and Sugget lifts one off the peg,
and Ellis Twistle rolls his own
and Butcher Boysie stirs his brawn
and Mrs Boot and Mr Boot
within the ancient corner shop
set out their stall of fancy goods,
behind the counter, in the dock.

JE's bedroom.

JE Don't fuss, woman. It's not like anyone can see me.

Rose That's not an excuse for untidiness. Right, that's your fringe out of your eyes. Do you want those hairs in your ears clipping?

JE Do I hell as like. It's a radio station I run, not telly. Anyway, where's Wesley?

Rose Pumping water onto a fire somewhere. His bleeper went off and he was out of that door like a scalded cat.

JE Well, God help the poor sod whose house is burning down when that wet lettuce turns up to put it out. Talk about pissing in the wind, he couldn't put out a candle, that lad.

Rose Oh leave him alone, John Edward. And watch your language will you, you get worse and worse.

JE I'm a man whose legs don't work, and now she wants to take away his tongue as well.

Rose And you can pipe down with self-pity because that doesn't impress either. Right, you're done.

JE Thanks, love. Rose?

Rose What?

JE Give us a kiss.

Rose Oh, we *are* honoured. (*Pecks him on the cheek.*)

JE You know he's back in town, don't you? Spoon, I mean.

Rose Yes, I know.

JE If he calls round, if he . . . you know . . . makes any moves . . . you will say, won't you?

Rose We're on one side of the road and he's on the other. End of story.

JE Right. Good. He's always had a shilling on himself, that one, but he's history as far as I'm concerned – never give him a minute's thought. Good. Right. If you'll just flick that switch, Rose, then you're excused.

Rose Don't mention it. And mind what I say, watch that tongue.

JE (*into radio mic*) Testing, testing, one, two, three, you're listening to Radio Castle, the voice of Jerusalem. Before the phone-in show, a special message: Jerusalem Social Club is sad to announce the retirement of its long-serving Entertainments Secretary Mr Alwin Wagstaff, to concentrate on his business interests. Well done, Alwin, a sterling effort, and we wish you many customers with more brass than brains in the years to come. This situation obviously leaves the position vacant, and I can now reveal that the principal candidate is none other than yours truly. That's right, folks, you heard it here live and exclusive. John Edward Castle for Entertainments Secretary, looking forward to your support in advance, and I'll be making regular election broadcasts right up until the vote, so stay tuned. Now, on with the show. First caller on line one, you're through to Radio Castle.

Caller 1 I'd like to report more animals going missing. Mi uncle's toy poodle, Killer, disappeared on Tuesday.

He's black but he does white poo, so you'd recognise him anywhere.

JE Yes, very bad this spate of animal thefts. Check the deep freeze in the Pearl of India is my advice, or that carvery in Todmorden. Line two?

Caller 2 Two koi carp missing from a fishpond in Globe Street.

JE Two glorified goldfish – keep an eye out, please. Any more animals? Line one?

Spoon Hello, John Edward. Mr Spoon here, your neighbour.

JE What do you want?

Spoon Just to wish you all the best in the election.

JE Oh, well, thank you. Much appreciated, I'm sure.

Spoon Yes, very exciting. Just what this town needs, a two-horse race.

JE Indeed, indeed. What? What do you mean, two-horse race? Says who?

Spoon Says me, John Edward, live and exclusive on Radio Castle. That's right folks, you heard it here first. Take Jerusalem out of the gloom – vote Spoon.

JE But . . . but . . . you can't, you're not even a member.

Spoon Life member, toast of the town after dragging a certain fireman out of a burning barn, if you remember back that far. Well, see you at the polling station.

JE (*screams*) NO. NO. Don't you dare hang up on me. You parasite. You sponge. Go against a man with no legs would you – that's just about your level. Well, I'll squash you, Spoon, I'll flatten you, you'll see . . .

Rose (*bursting into room*) What is it, John, what's all the fuss?

JE You leech, you bloodsucking creep, I'll grind you into the dirt, I'll crush you, Spoon, I'll chew you up and spit you out again, I'll break you into a million little pieces, you'll be mush, you'll be pulp, I'll pulverise you, you vermin, you rodent, you shite. You'll see, Spoon, you'll be nothing but mush, mush, mush . . .

He dissolves into sobs, comforted by Rose.

Narrator
      A wind of change, a change in the weather.
      And the weathervane with its iron finger
      twists and turns on the Town Hall roof
      like the hand of God in search of the truth,
      and finally swivels around to the future,
      and points to a date we should all remember:
      Election Day, on the fifth of November.

Act Two

Narrator
>So under a sky that pours and pours,
>Wesley Castle goes door-to-door,
>taking his father out to the people,
>bringing John Edward down to street level.

*In Jerusalem town. Wesley enters tobacconist's shop –
bell rings.*

Wesley Mr Twistle?

Twistle Ah, young Wesley.

Wesley Not so young any more, I'm afraid. Anyway, mi dad's sent you this.

Twistle That would be a cauliflower, *Brassica oleracea botrytis*?

Wesley Yeah, although it's better known by its common name: a bribe. I've to tell you that he's looking forward to your support in the forthcoming election.

Twistle I see. Well, food for thought, quite literally. Tell him I'm a floating voter. Tell him a nice firm cabbage wouldn't do any harm either.

Wesley I'll tell him. See you later.

*

Wesley Oi, you two. Mi dad says he's thinking of having the roof felted and the slates turned. He's wondering if you want the work?

Beardsley 1 Aye, we could give him a price. Wouldn't be cheap, mind. You've got your materials and your labour.

Beardsley 2 And that's before you've even started.

Wesley I'm pretty sure if you can both put a cross next to his name on polling day then he'd be willing to put his hand into his pocket. Know what I mean?

Beardsley 1 Tell him the roof's worth one vote. For two he might need his chimney lining as well.

Wesley I'll tell him.

*

Sugget 1 Master Castle, if I'm not mistaken. Will it be made-to-measure or something from the rail?

Sugget 2 What about this nice double-breasted in brush-velvet?

Wesley No thanks, fellers, I've just come with a message from mi dad. He says wouldn't it look good for Sugget and Sugget if he were seen to be wearing one of your suits on his election posters? End of message.

Sugget 1 Tell Mr Castle Senior, from each according to his ability . . .

Sugget 2 . . . to each according to his needs.

Wesley I'll tell him.

Sugget 1 Oh Wesley, no offence, but he won't be wanting the full suit will he? Just the jacket, presumably?

Wesley (*answering mobile phone*) What? I'm on mi way, aren't I? Look, Dad, I didn't want to do this in the first place – you should do your own dirty work. Yes, I understand what it means for the good name of the family, all I'm saying is I'll be a lot quicker if you leave me alone to get on with it.

JE's bedroom.

JE (*putting phone down*) Leave you to get on with it and you'd still be lying in bed pulling your pudding. Useless lump. About as much use as a . . . (*Farts loudly.*) Oh, speak up Brown, you're through. Right then, showtime. (*into radio microphone*) Testing, testing, one, two, three, you're listening to Radio Castle, the voice of Jerusalem, and we begin this morning with an election broadcast on behalf of yours truly, Mr John Edward Castle. Now I know what some of you are thinking – how can a man like him, injured in a legendary act of heroism, a man now paying a lifetime's price for one moment of bravery, a man . . .

Nurse (*pops her head round door*) Mr Castle, there was no answer . . . I've come to look at those pressure-sores.

JE Get out, you daft cow, I'm on the air!

Nurse (*retreating*) Sorry, sorry.

JE Er . . . a man locked in an endless arm-wrestle with the cruel hand of fate . . . how can he be Jerusalem Social Club's new Entertainments Secretary? Well, let me put your minds at rest, voters. With a combination of modern technology and good old human endeavour, I'll be right with you every minute of the day, booking acts on the phone, compering over the PA, listening in on a microphone, and my piece de resistance . . . nothing less than a video link-up on Saturday nights, calling out your numbers from right here at Castle HQ. So don't forget: FOR PEACE OF MIND AND ZERO HASSLE, VOTE FOR LOCAL HERO CASTLE! Stay tuned to this frequency for further bulletins, and look out for our Wesley – he'll be paying you all a house call. That concludes this election broadcast. And now for some music.

Narrator
> And up on the heath above streets and people,
> out through clouds comes the sight of a man
> like an astronaut steering his lunar module:
> it's Spoon, on his own, in his Transit van,
> lost in his world, in his own little bubble.

Driving along in van.

Spoon (*singing*) 'For those in peril on the sea . . .' (*Opens letter with teeth, reads while driving.*)

'Dear Mr Spoon, you are hereby invited to participate in a live election debate at Jerusalem Social Club on the evening of November 4th. Your opponent in the contest, Mr John Edward Castle, will be appearing courtesy of Wagstaff's Televisual Emporium Ltd – for all your viewing requirements at competitive prices. Yours sincerely, Alwin Wagstaff, Entertainments Secretary. PS. Please let me know by return of post whether you intend to take part.'

Oh, I'll be there, don't you worry about that. I wouldn't miss it for . . .

Car swerves.

Oh my God. (*Gets out of car.*) Rose? Rose? Oh God, oh my God, Rose are you in there, can you hear me, Rose?

Rose Over here.

Spoon Rose, thank God. I thought you were trapped in there. What happened?

Rose I must have been daydreaming. One minute I was driving along, the next I was sliding off into the ditch.

Spoon Did you go through the windscreen?

Rose No, but a tub of dog biscuits did. I just climbed out in a daze, then I came and sat under this tree, just thinking what a nice view it is.

Spoon Put my jacket around you. You've got a cut on your forehead, let me see to it with this hankie.

Rose I was just making a delivery, running late as usual –

Spoon Rose, when I saw the car in the ditch, I just can't tell you how much I . . . I'm sorry, I can't help it.

Rose Why did you come back?

Spoon A whim, really. I've got nothing else, only the past. I didn't intend buying the house right across the road, but when it was up for sale, it just felt like fate. Do you want me to leave Jerusalem? Say so, and I will.

Rose No, don't leave. It's just that . . . you and John Edward. Why do you taunt each other like you do?

Spoon Two big babies, I suppose, both squabbling over the same toy.

Rose Is that what I am? A plaything.

Spoon I didn't mean it like that. I'm sorry, I'm not much good at saying the right thing any more. It's what comes of being on your own for too long.

Rose Don't think it's just you.

Spoon What do you mean?

Rose You're not the only who's lonely.

Spoon Rose . . .

Rose You're not the only one who needs some contact. (*She reaches for his hand, puts it inside her coat and folds her arms across her chest.*)

Spoon Rose, Rose . . .

Rose It's so complicated.

Spoon I know, I know. I'll keep my distance, unless you tell me otherwise. I just feel so attached to you, I always have.

Rose How attached do you want to get?

Spoon Very. Completely.

Rose OK. How about now?

Spoon You mean . . . right this minute?

Rose Close – that's what you want, isn't it? Joined together?

Spoon You mean . . . here?

Rose Right here, right now.

Spoon Well, I . . .

Rose Come on, let's do it. Get that rope out of the van, tie it to my car and you can tow me back into town.

Spoon (*laughing*) Rose.

Rose Here, have a Canine Crunchy.

Spoon Are they fit for human consumption?

Rose Well, they never do John Edward any harm.

SCENE THREE

Narrator
And a flock of doves that came to feed
on the scattered crumbs of biscuit and seed
now lifts and climbs of its own accord
like a kite, like a thought, like a flag, like a sign,
and leaves those love-birds minding their own

on the edge of the moor, at the side of the road. Meanwhile, down in the town . . .

Gert Castle's house. Doorstep.

Gert Whatever you're flogging I don't want any.

Census Taker Census, ma'am. Just need to ask a few questions.

Gert Like what?

Census Taker Name?

Gert Gert Castle.

Census Taker Ah, you must be John Edward's mother. It was only the other day I was talking to your grandson, Wesley, about . . .

Gert Cut the flimflam, laddie. I'll say it once – so write it down then piss off. I'm Gert Castle, I'm a widow, and my dear departed was Jerusalem's greatest fireman, just like my son, and just like his son if he'd get his act together. I get fire-service pension which is fuck-all, whoever comes visiting is no business of yours, and don't ask me my age or you'll get a smack in the gob. Now hop it.

Census Taker Er, one last question. Any pets?

Gert I've got a pig if you must know.

Census Taker I see – so you've got a smallholding somewhere, have you?

Gert No lad, he's hanging up by his heels in the pantry with his throat cut and bucket under his chin to catch the blood. Now, unless it's a pork pie you're after, I'm sure you've got better things to do, and I know I have, so sling your hook.

JE (*walkie-talkie in Gert's house*) Mother, can you hear me? Mother? Have you got me switched on?

Gert Course I can hear you. What do you want?

JE I was just looking out of the telescope and saw a man at your door. Wondered if you were alright?

Gert Just some nosy-parker from the council. And when I want Neighbourhood Watch I'll damn well ask for it, OK? Also, just because your father's dead doesn't mean my sex drive is, so you keep your beady eye on your doorstep and never mind who crosses mine, comprende?

JE Yes, Mother.

Gert You've enough on your own plate with that Spoon character – you want to watch him, the slimeball. And while we're on the subject, what about Wesley?

JE What about him?

Gert Get him whipped into line. Tell him to get signed up full-time instead of playing at it. Half-hearted, he is, in more ways than one.

JE What's that supposed to mean?

Gert You know damn well what I mean. Does he have a girlfriend, or is he one of them artistic types, because if he is, that explains everything.

JE Mother!

Gert Sitting up there on your arse all day doesn't mean you can duck out of it. You're his father, aren't you? Get some fathering done.

JE Yes, Mother.

Gert Now is that it, or did you want something else?

JE No, nothing.

Gert Good, because these animals need their dinner.
Over and out.

JE's bedroom.

JE (*switching off intercom*) Over and out, Mother dear.
(*Adjusts himself in bed. Drinks glass of beer. Farts
loudly.*) Don't tear it, madam, I'll take it whole. (*into mic*)
This is Radio Castle with the bingo session. A pound for
a line, three pounds for a full house. Five pounds jackpot
for under sixty numbers. Phone in on the Bingo Hotline
when you're up. No time wasters please. There's a pound
fine for any false calls, all proceeds to Jerusalem Fire
Brigade, such as it is now, and God knows they need all
the help they can get. Eyes down for your next five
numbers: three and four, thirty-four; two and eight,
twenty-eight; Heinz Varieties, five and seven, fifty-seven;
legs eleven – (*Wolf-whistles.*) Thank you, whistlers, what
a smasher, two fried eggs and a gammon rasher; four and
eight, forty-eight. Any takers? Hard luck, folks, but tune
in again in an hour for your next five numbers, and a
cash prize might be winging its way to your pocket! (*into
Tannoy*) Wesley, are you downstairs? Come up here,
I want a word with you.

Wesley (*entering room*) What's up? I need to get these
books back to the library.

JE The library doesn't close for another hour. Now just
reach up into that cupboard will you, and get me that
box.

Wesley This shoebox?

JE That's it. Tip it open on the bed. There. Have you
seen those before?

Wesley No. What are they, medals from the war?

JE Decorations, son, that's what they are, and they're your inheritance. Fire-service medals, won by me, and won by your grandfather, for bravery and duty. Go on, pick them up, feel them in your hands.

Wesley They could do with a bit of a polish.

JE They could do with adding to, more like, and that's your responsibility.

Wesley I'm hardly going to qualify for the George Cross as a volunteer, am I? We only get called out a couple of times a week, and that's to pull a hedgehog out of a blocked drain.

JE Aye, but if you joined up full-time, in Halifax or even Leeds?

Wesley Dad, I've got a job, with the Water Board.

JE Precisely. Wrong element, you see. Us Castles have got fire in our blood. You've gone about things the wrong way round, seen it from the wrong end. I only hope you don't see everything from that side.

Wesley Meaning what, exactly?

JE Don't you think it's time you got yourself a girlfriend? People are going to be talking.

Wesley Oh yeah, and what will they be saying? That John Edward Castle fathered a queer – is that what you're worried about?

JE The first person who says that gets banjaxed, alright? I might be crippled and trapped up here in this room, but I'm more of a man than anyone out there, more than a match for all of them put together, and if you had any spine you'd be acting like a man as well, instead of poncing around up at that reservoir, fiddling about with . . .

Wesley That's it, Dad. (*He storms out.*) Conversation finished. I'm off.

JE Wesley, come back here, I haven't said what I meant to say. Wesley? (*Pause.*) It's not easy trying to be a dad like this, you know, stuck in this bed or this chair. I'm sorry, alright? Wesley! (*Pause.*) God, messed it up again. Oh, the daft lump's forgotten his library books. Let's have a look what he's reading, see if I can get on his wavelength. What the . . . *The Emergency Services: a Marxist Approach* by Sinclair O'Toole. *Pump or Penis: a Feminist Interpretation of Fire-Fighting* . . . I don't believe it. I just don't believe it. (*Pushes himself over to window and opens it.*) Wesley, you've forgotten something. (*Throws books out of window.*) And don't you ever, ever bring that kind of rubbish into this house again. You're a disgrace. Do you hear me? You make me cringe.

SCENE FOUR

Narrator
　　　Later that day on the reservoir bank,
　　　maggots are threaded on silver hooks
　　　and lines are loaded with lead, and sink
　　　to where slippery creatures slink and skulk,
　　　perch and carp, trout and chub,
　　　and above the fish, from separate rods,
　　　two floats entwine and tangle up.

Spoon Sorry, the current must have got it. Anyway, you're the first thing I've caught all day.

Wesley Yeah, not having much luck myself.

Spoon You're John Edward's son, aren't you?

Wesley For mi sins. It's Mr Spoon isn't it, you've just moved in across the road? I heard about you and mi mother.

Spoon What?

Wesley Getting hitched up.

Spoon Well, I . . .

Wesley About towing her home after she skidded in the car. Thanks for doing that.

Spoon Oh, I see. A pleasure. Not a problem.

Wesley So do you come here a lot?

Spoon I haven't done for a good few years, but it's a perfect spot.

Wesley There's nothing better than staring at the water, letting the world drift by. I don't like fire – it leaps up into the air. It's out of control. I like water. It stays on the ground. Finds its own level.

Spoon Yes, fishing – it's like . . . happiness. (*Following up his line of thought.*) The best fish lie in the deepest, calmest water, but to get at them you have to disturb the surface.

Wesley (*encouraged by Spoon's philosophy*) Yes, yes, that's fascinating. Freud's very interesting on the subject, don't you find?

Spoon Freud?

Wesley Yes, fluidity and so on. It's maternal, of course. The subconscious, the transforming ocean, the boundless sea. And the womb, obviously, the intrauterine birth and the breaking of the water.

Spoon Oh yes. Obviously.

Wesley Now, in Jungian symbolism, fire is the antithesis of water – consuming and destructive and masculine. It can be made as well, conjured out of the air, turning mortals into gods. And of course it's the libido – that goes without saying, right?

Spoon opens his mouth but nothing comes out.

I bet you're a Piscean. Are you? Pisces?

Spoon Oh, no, I'm a Leo.

Wesley Oh, well, I am anyway. That's why I've got fish on the brain, I reckon. Yeah, fishing – it's pretty much all I think about these days.

Spoon Well, there's worse things you can do with a long stick and a worm.

Wesley You're a policeman, aren't you? Have you come back to investigate all those stolen animals in town?

Spoon No, I retired a long time ago, in another life.

Wesley How long ago?

Spoon Oh, I'm going back twenty-four years now.

Wesley Oh, nineteen-seventy . . .

Spoon Er, yes, whatever. Before your time.

Wesley I know you're standing against mi dad, in the election. Well, just to say that it doesn't bother me. I'm not mithered either way. Maybe we could go fishing again?

Spoon (*puts his hand on Wesley's shoulder*) I'd like that very much, son. I'll look forward to it. Well, I've got some electioneering to do, I'm afraid. See you around.

Wesley Yes. See you around. (*Carries on fishing.*) Nineteen seventy-nine. (*Threads line, casts out, sits down.*) Year I was born.

Narrator
So the tide rises, and the tide falls.
And the clocks go back as the nights draw in,
and dusk comes hard on the heels of dawn,
and bonfires wait to be stacked and torched,
and we come to the night of November the fourth.
A packed house at Jerusalem Social Club,
a sea of faces down in the hall
in a steamy, beery, smoky fug.

Jerusalem Social Club

Wagstaff Ladies and gentlemen, best of order if you please. We all know why we're here, so let's get on with it. I'm sure neither candidate needs introducing, but I'll introduce them in any case, beginning with Mr Spoon on my right.

Spoon Good evening.

Wagstaff And on my left, er, in spirit if not in body, Mr John Edward Castle. Can you hear me, JE? JE, can you hear me?

Beardsley 1 (*from the back of the hall*) Ground Control to Major Tom.

Much laughter in the hall.

Wagstaff Best of order, please. Best of order. Can anybody sort this thing out?

Wesley (*shouting from the audience*) Just twiddle that knob. No, the one on the left, that's it.

Wagstaff We've started, JE. Lift off. You're on the air.

JE (*TV screen*) Oh, er, er, good evening everybody. (*He is obviously reading from a script.*) Friends, family and acquaintances, I'd like to begin by thanking you for giving up your valuable time this evening to come and see things as they really are.

Wagstaff Thank you, JE.

JE Now, it's my opinion, and one which I share with all right-minded people of this town, that the position of Entertainments Secretary is a position of honour and responsibility, and with this in mind I've put my own name forward, as a man who's lived and breathed Jerusalem since the day he was born – (*getting angry*) and not some fly-by-night, here one minute and gone the next . . .

Wesley (*to Rose, under his breath*) It's a nightmare.

Rose He hasn't even warmed up yet.

Gert Oh, shut up for God's sake, JE, or we'll be here till midnight.

Wagstaff Thank you, JE. And thank you, Gert.

Gert My pleasure, lover boy.

Wagstaff Er, yes. Well, without further ado, then, does anyone have any questions?

Beardsley 1 Wor about doffers?

Wagstaff I beg your pardon, Mr Beardsley?

Beardsley 1 Wor about doffers? Strippers?

Wagstaff What about them?

Beardsley 1 Will we have 'em, or won't we?

Wagstaff I see. I'll put that question to Mr Castle first. JE, as I understand it the question is as follows: should you be elected, would you be inviting strippers to come and . . . er . . . perform at the club?

JE Well, as far as I'm concerned it's just a bit of harmless fun, isn't it? Always has been, always will.

Noreen It's a disgrace.

Lots of agreement amongst the women.

JE (*flustered*) It's not something I'd be interested in personally, obviously, but it's traditional, isn't it, and if somebody wants to get their kit off on stage, she can do, and those who want to watch can watch, and those who don't want to don't have to. Yes. Thank you.

Rose (*to Wesley*) Nude women? He'd run a mile.

Wesley Aye, if he could.

Rose Wesley!

Wagstaff Best of order, please. Mr Spoon?

Spoon (*composed*) Male or female, Mr Beardsley? Which are you interested in?

A great roar of laughter.

In my view, it's the feeling of the membership that counts, not just the opinion of one man. But I will say this: Jerusalem Social Club has a reputation second to none, and a waiting list that reflects that reputation. I should also say that we shouldn't ask anyone to do anything that we wouldn't be prepared to do ourselves, so unless one or both of the Beardsley Brothers want to come up here and show us what they have in mind . . .

Uproar and cheers in the hall.

Wagstaff Father Noah, your question please.

Fr Noah I should like to ask Mr Spoon and Mr Castle about the quality of entertainment we can expect to see at the club.

Wagstaff Mr Spoon?

Spoon During the years I've been away from Jerusalem, I built up a successful chauffeur and escort service – looking after some very big names, making arrangements for tours, hospitality and suchlike. If it's admissible, I'd like to offer this letter, just as a taste of things to come.

Wagstaff (*opening and reading letter*) 'My dear Mr Spoon. Just a short note to thank you for all your endless patience and dedicated professionalism, and for making my tour a very smooth and successful one. If I can ever repay the favour, please don't hesitate to ask. Yours affectionately, Shirley . . .'

(*to Spoon*) I can't quite make out the signature.

Spoon Bassey, I think you'll find. Shirley Bassey.

Uproar again in the hall, lots of excitement.

JE I don't believe it.

Wagstaff (*sniffing*) Perfumed as well.

Rose Shirley Bassey?

Wesley Mum, what's wrong?

Gert It's rubbish. All rubbish. Tell him, John.

JE Oh very smart, Spoon, very smart. But don't think we don't know what's going on. You think you can come here with your fancy talk and fancy letters, and pull the wool over everybody's eyes, don't you? Well, let me tell you, you've got it wrong. All wrong. This isn't the London Palladium, and I don't care if you've got promises from Elvis Presley or Jesus Christ for that matter, because they're not needed.

Rose (*shouting out*) John, will you calm down, you'll make yourself poorly.

Gert Let him talk, woman.

JE Tradition, that's what this club's built on. Bingo Friday and Saturday night, a singer or comic from Leeds or Bradford, the odd country and western night, discos, race trips, raffles, a bit of supper . . . that's what people want. Am I right, everybody? You tell him, you tell him that's what you want.

Silence in the hall.

Noreen Have you really met Shirley Bassey?

Spoon Well, I . . .

JE Has he bollocks like. And what do we care if he has? What do we care if he's met Shirley MacLaine or Shirley bloody Temple. We don't need 'em. Shirley Bassey my cock. Who's he going to bring up next? Tom Jones?

Spoon Actually, its funny that you should mention Tom, because it was only last week . . .

Noreen If he can get Tom Jones, he's good enough for me!

Rose That's it. I'm off.

Wesley Mum. Shall I come with you?

Rose No, stay here and sweep up the glass.

Wesley What glass?

Gert Come on then, all of you. I'll take you all on, you bunch of cunts . . .

A glass gets thrown. Chaos breaks out in the hall. More glasses are thrown.

Wagstaff People, please. Best of order. This is Jerusalem, not Beirut, not Manchester.

Outside. Rain. Spoon running after Rose.

Spoon Rose, come back. Where are you going?

Rose Home to my husband, who you've just humiliated.

Spoon Well, take this brolly at least, it's pouring down.

Rose I'd rather drown. Why don't you give it to *Shirley* – I'm sure she wouldn't want to get her hair wet.

Wesley has run after his mother and overhears their conversation. He hides/shelters in a phone box, still listening.

Spoon Oh come on, Rose.

Rose And that jacket you put round me the other week, I suppose you spread that over a puddle for her, did you?

Spoon I'm flattered.

Rose What the hell does that mean?

Spoon That you think someone like her could be remotely interested in me.

Rose Well, don't be flattered. Your fancy stories don't impress me, Spoon.

Spoon It was a lie – alright. He goaded me into it. Look, Rose. Rose – look at these hands – five years on a trawler in the North Atlantic. You don't get skin like this holding hands with Shirley Bassey.

Rose Well, you might have taken that lot in but I can see right through you.

Spoon I wish you could, Rose, then you'd be able to see what's inside me. There's only one heart and mind I want to win over and that's yours. That's how it was before, and it hasn't changed.

Rose I'm not listening.

Spoon It's what I wanted twenty-four years ago, and for a few beautiful weeks it was what you wanted as well. And it's what you want now, isn't it? Isn't it? ISN'T IT?

Rose I need to go home. Here, keep your brolly, it's a long walk in the rain.

Spoon A long walk to where?

Rose Wherever you're going, away from here. Goodbye, Spoon.

Wesley comes out of the phone box, from where he has overheard their conversation. He stands in the rain in the empty street. He examines two election posters on the wall, one of JE and one of Spoon, studying their facial characteristics. He goes back into the call box.

Wesley (*to himself*) Twenty-four years ago. Nineteen seventy-nine. Year I was born.

He goes back into the phone box to shelter from the rain and sees a number on a card. After a while he calls it.

Hello, is that the Samaritans?

Samaritan Yes it is, how can I help you?

Wesley Er, well, I'm just ringing on behalf of a friend, really. He was wondering, it's only a theory, like, but what if he'd just found out that his dad isn't his dad really, or not his proper dad anyway, and I . . . he . . . was just wondering whether or not he should feel sad, because I don't think he does feel sad, although he might do later, and whether he might want to throw himself

47

off a bridge, and if he did, could you recommend any good ones, or what to do if he gets drunk and joins the Foreign Legion accidentally. I mean, he's already in the fire brigade and he can't even deal with that, so what chance is there?

Samaritan Is that Wesley? Wesley Castle?

Wesley Er, no. It's somebody else.

Samaritan Wesley, it's Sarah from school. Sarah Stranks. I'd recognise your voice anywhere.

Wesley Oh, er, Sarah. Yeah, sorry, I was just making a hoax call. You know, for a bet?

Sarah So are you married now, Wesley?

Wesley Er, not especially.

Sarah Alright, here's my advice. Go to the Pearl of India in about thirty minutes, get a nice candlelit table and order a bottle of wine.

Wesley And will that do the trick?

Sarah No, but I will when I turn up to meet you. How does that sound?

Wesley Er, well, aren't you supposed to . . . er, what do you mean?

Sarah I'm asking you out on a date, you clot.

Wesley Are you? Wow. Thanks. I mean . . . yes. I didn't know the Samaritans offered such a comprehensive service.

Sarah They don't, but I've always had a soft spot for you, so I'm taking advantage while you're depressed. Anyway, I've just been on an assertiveness training course. See you there.

Wesley See you there. (*Puts phone down.*) Blimey. (*His bleeper goes off.*) Oh f . . .

Narrator
    . . . fire in the hole, all hands to the pump.

    And the weathervane with its iron finger
    twists and turns on the Town Hall roof
    like the hand of God in search of the truth,
    and swivels around to a date in the future:
    Election Day, on the fifth of November,
    coming nearer and nearer . . .

Act Three

JE's bedroom

JE (*into radio mic*) You're listening to Radio Castle, the voice of Jerusalem – I'll just take a couple more calls. Yes, line one, you're on the air.

Caller It's about all these animals going missing. I left the kitchen window open yesterday, and when I got back from the shops somebody had nicked off with my budgie cage.

JE Outrageous. You did the right thing to call me about it. I presume this cage had a budgie in it, did it?

Caller No, it had a lemon sponge cake in it. Course it had a budgie in it, you stupid man, that's what budgie cages are for, you don't think I'd . . .

JE Thank you, caller. Line two?

Caller Yeah, I've got a plan about how to stop this animal thief. You get a goat to swallow a couple of pounds of explosives and a detonator, right, then tie it up on the putting green one night. Thief comes and takes it, then you blow it up using a remote control, right, and whoever you find on the end of a rope covered in goat guts and whatever – that's your man.

JE Thank you, caller, I can see you've thought long and hard about that. Right, the last item of the day is an election broadcast on behalf of myself. People, you won't need reminding that today's the day, a straight choice between me and the loathsome Mr Spoon. (*Spits.*) Now I might be a man in a wheelchair –

Violins start playing.

– a man who looks longingly from his bedroom window every day of his life as others stroll, arm in arm through the streets and birds fly free through the air, a man you could weep for . . . but I don't want your sympathy –

Music stops.

– I want your vote. So get down to that club and do the decent thing. FOR PEACE OF MIND AND ZERO HASSLE, VOTE FOR LOCAL HERO CASTLE. Tune in tomorrow for the results and a victory speech to remember. (*Switches off mike, farts loudly.*) Oh, the Kraken wakes.

Banging on wall.

Wesley (*knocking on the door*) Dad.

JE What do you want?

Wesley (*entering the room*) Just wondered what you were up to?

JE I'm just ready to set off on a triathlon. What do you think, I'm bloody well up to? Fuck all, as per.

Wesley Oh, OK.

JE Go on.

Wesley What?

JE What do you want?

Wesley Well, er, tell me to mind mi own business, but when you got injured, did it stop anything working, apart from your legs, you know, did it . . . affect anything else?

JE Such as?

Wesley Come on, don't make me say it.

JE It couldn't have, could it, or you wouldn't be around to ask such a stupid question. Subject closed. Now, if you don't mind, I've got these opinion polls to look at.

Wesley Right. Right.

JE (*softer*) Er, listen. You, er, know what day it is, don't you?

Wesley Yeah, it's the election.

JE November the fifth, Bonfire night. That's when I copped this lot, you know.

Wesley Yeah, I know.

JE Twenty-five years ago to the day. Flames coming from every window, roof on fire, but you know what – I never thought twice, I was straight in there, looking for that child, doing my job.

Wesley I know, Dad. We all know. You were very brave.

JE Anyhow, be careful. You're bound to get called out, and we don't want two cripples in the family. Who's going to take my bets down to the bookies if you can't, eh?

Wesley I'll be careful.

Rose (*coming into room*) John, here's your lunch. Do you want it in the chair or in bed?

JE Just put it down there, I'll eat it later.

Rose Oh, Wesley, someone called Sarah phoned.

Wesley Sarah Stranks?

JE A female, eh? Good lad.

Rose I forgot to get her number. I phoned that 1471 thing but it was the Samaritans – that can't be right, can it?

Wesley's bleeper goes off.

Wesley (*under his breath*) Saved by the bell.

JE Go on, lad, get on that pump. And mind what I said.

Wesley (*rushing out*) I will. See you later.

Narrator
> Meanwhile,
> through the iron gates of Jerusalem's graveyard
> here comes a man with a government clipboard.

Census Taker (*writing in notebook*) Two-thirty p.m., vicar not at vicarage, advised by cleaner to try church. (*Knocks on door of church and goes in.*) Hello, Father. Hello. Hello.

Fr Noah (*coming down aisle to meet him*) Hello, young man. Just topping up the communion wine and er – (*Burps.*) one or two other things. Can I help?

Census Taker Census taker. I just need your details, if you don't mind. Your cleaner said I'd find you here.

Fr Noah Oh yes, it may be the house of God but it's home from home for me. Well, I'm Father Noah, vicar of the Parish of Jerusalem. Single man but looking for the right woman, sole resident of Jerusalem vicarage, and no dependants, other than my flock, of course.

Census Taker Keep sheep, do you?

Fr Noah My congregation. Small but perfectly formed, and loyal to their shepherd.

Census Taker On the subject of animals, do you have any pets?

Fr Noah A few mice in the vestry, that's all. Will there be anything else?

Census Taker It's just that . . . someone mentioned they'd seen a horse in the church. And a donkey as well, and a couple of cows in fact. And a pig.

Fr Noah Ah, that's true, I have to confess. And you'd like to see them, would you?.

Census Taker If you wouldn't mind.

Father Noah whips a cloth away from a Nativity scene. Several toy animals are congregated around the infant Christ in the manger.

Fr Noah If it's those missing animals you're interested in, I'm afraid you're barking up the wrong tree. Noah's the name, but this is a church – not an ark – and I'm not expecting rain.

Census Taker Sorry to have troubled you.

Fr Noah Not at all. There's a collection tray just on your left next to the hymn books. (*Goes off singing.*)

'All things bright and beautiful, all creatures . . .'

SCENE THREE

Narrator
> Light the blue fuse and stand well back.
> Never return to a burning squib.
> And later that night there's a smell in the air –
> it's the stench of smoke, the stink of fire,
> like touch-paper fuming down to the quick,
> like the smouldering of a powder keg.
> On the steps of Jerusalem Social Club,
> Mr Spoon, in the midst of his gunpowder plot,
> is meeting his public, picking them off.

Outside the Social Club.

Spoon Hello, Cecil, coming to vote?

Cecil That's what it looks like.

Spoon I was going through some old police files the other day. Should have handed them in when I retired, but some things always end up in the back of the wardrobe. Anyway, I came across those photographs of yours we had to confiscate. Self-portraits, weren't they?

Cecil The charges were dropped.

Spoon They were. Still, it would be a shame if they ever saw the light of day, now you've moved up in the world. Amazing detail – that cactus must have hurt, though, didn't it? And was that yoghurt, or fromage frais?

Cecil Alright, Spoon. I get the message. I'll vote for you.

*

Spoon Boysie the Butcher. How's the meat trade?

Boysie Ay, mustn't crumble, as one mad cow said to another.

Spoon Actually, I was thinking the other day that what this club needs, along with decent entertainment, is a new attitude towards catering. Know what I mean? If I'm elected, the first thing I'll be looking at is someone to supply good quality meat on a regular basis, if you get my drift.

Boysie Nod's as good as a wink to a veal calf.

*

Spoon Jalopy Joe.

Jalopy Joe Spoon. How's that van of yours going on?

Spoon On its last legs. In fact, if all goes to plan, I'm going to be needing something a bit more upmarket, something with a bit of class. Can't be going down to the station to pick up the talent in an old Transit, can I? Joe?

Jalopy Joe Say no more.

SCENE FOUR

JE's room, a Super-8 cine-film playing against the wall.

JE Where was this, was it Scarborough?

Rose Bridlington. On the front.

JE Look at that mangy donkey. Pathetic.

Rose Poor thing.

JE That sea looks cold.

Rose Didn't you do some fishing off the pier?

JE Fishing? Me? No. You're confusing me with someone else.

Rose Oh. Er . . . we were staying at that guest house, don't you remember?

JE Which one?

Rose The one with the electric meters in the bedrooms and the ten o'clock curfew. Horrible it was, but it was all we could afford. Single rooms as well, or at least that's what we had to tell my mother.

JE Look at that donkey. I've seen more hair on a monkey's bum.

Rose We'd been going out two years. Single rooms my foot. It would have taken more than a partition wall to keep you out at that time, I can tell you.

JE Alright, Rose. No need to rub it in.

56

Rose No need to rub what in?

JE About . . . sexual relations and all that. By the time I've got out of this bloody chair and unplugged all the pipes I'm not exactly in the mood. It's humiliating.

Rose What about me? I'm human as well, I've got needs, I'm not a bloody mermaid. (*Pause.*) Sorry. I just thought it would be nice to see some of those old films, that's all. Something we could do together.

JE Hmm. I suppose.

Downstairs.

Spoon knocks on the door and goes in. He hears the rest of Rose and JE's coversation through the Tannoy, which has been left on.

Spoon Hello, Rose. Anyone at home. Hello? Hello?

Rose (*Tannoy*) It's not easy, not easy for either of us.

JE (*Tannoy*) No.

Rose (*Tannoy*) But we've made it this far, haven't we?

JE (*Tannoy*) Yes, we have. I'm not sure how sometimes, but we have.

Rose (*Tannoy*) Well, we're a family, aren't we?

JE (*Tannoy*) You know, Rose, I'd give anything for it not to be sat here with wires and tubes sticking out, sat in this room for the rest of my life.

Rose (*Tannoy*) But we're always offering to take you out in the wheelchair.

JE (*Tannoy*) I couldn't bear it – like some big baby in his pram. (*tearful*) I'd rather they remembered me the way

57

I was, I'd rather *you* remembered me the way I was. Not coming in here having to bath me and cut my toenails.

Rose (*Tannoy*) I know, I know. Come here, don't get upset.

JE (*Tannoy*) It's not human. I should have died.

Rose (*Tannoy*) Come on now.

JE (*Tannoy*) How can you still love me when I'm like this? Tell me, Rose, do you still love me?

Rose (*Tannoy*) I'm your wife aren't I?

JE (*Tannoy*) You're my wife and I'm your husband.

Spoon (*to himself*) Oh God. Forgive me.

Wesley comes in through the front door

Wesley, er, I just called round and I heard voices, and thought there was somebody in.

Wesley They must be upstairs. I suppose you want my mum.

Spoon Er, no, I was popping in to remind everyone to vote. Look, this probably isn't a good time. I'll get off.

Spoon leaves. The outside door closes. Rose comes into the downstairs room from upstairs.

Rose Did I hear voices? Wesley, what are you doing in your uniform, haven't you been back to the station? And what's that, a black eye? Has there been an accident?

Wesley No. I've been sent home.

Rose What do you mean, sent home? What do you mean, Wesley?

JE (*Tannoy*) Wesley, is that you?

Wesley There was a fire in the school, some kids playing with fireworks. Smoke everywhere, and flames. They got

58

the turntable ladder out and told me to go up. I couldn't even see the end of it – just swirling smoke miles up in the sky. I got mi foot on the first rung, then I just froze.

Rose Oh, Wesley.

Wesley I couldn't do it, Mum. I don't like fire and I don't like heights. The chief ripped mi mask off, called me a chicken and smacked me in the face. Told me I'm finished.

Rose Oh Wes. I'm sorry.

JE (*Tannoy*) What was it, lad? Bonfire gone up early was it, or just a dog with its tail on fire? Come on, son, tell your old man.

Wesley Can you hear me?

JE (*Tannoy*) Loud and clear.

Wesley I've been sacked.

JE (*Tannoy*) You've been what?

Wesley Sacked. Finished. Laid off. Given the elbow. Sent for an early bath.

JE (*Tannoy*) What are you talking about, sacked? Didn't you get there in time? I told you to get a moped, not that bike.

Wesley Oh, I got there alright. Fire in the school. And I wouldn't go up the ladder. So I've been sent home.

JE (*Tannoy*) Wouldn't go in?

Wesley (*expecting compassion*) It was like you said, Dad. Explosions going off everywhere. I kept thinking about what you told me – to watch out. That's when I knew I couldn't do it.

JE (*Tannoy*) But . . . why not?

Wesley I was . . . you know.

JE (*Tannoy*) What?

Wesley Terrified.

JE (*Tannoy*) Terrified?

Wesley Terrified. Frightened. Scared.

JE (*Tannoy, exploding*) I knew it. I knew it. You make me sick, you great big marshmallow. You're pathetic, do you hear me, pathetic. Call yourself a fireman – you're a disgrace to the uniform, and now you've disgraced me as well.

Rose John, stop it.

JE (*Tannoy*) You keep out of it. I don't know how you've got the nerve to come home. Well, I'll tell you something, I'm twice, three times the man that you'll ever be, even stuck up here needing my teeth cleaned and my arse wiped. You're nothing, do you hear me, nothing.

Wesley Oh, and you love it don't you, lying there licking your wounds? You've wallowed in that bed for twenty-odd years because you haven't got the guts to fight it, and you've poisoned everybody else at the same time, and we're all sick and tired of it.

JE (*Tannoy*) Shut your mouth you . . . pimple. You're a disgrace to the family. I disown you.

Wesley Well, why doesn't that surprise me?

JE (*Tannoy*) Get up these stairs and we'll sort it out once and for all. Me and you, come on.

Wesley Don't be ridiculous.

JE (*Tannoy*) No, you won't, will you? I've always had you down as a commie and a ponce, but you're worse than that, you're a chicken.

Wesley Shut up, you pig. Shut up.

Rose Wesley, that's the Tannoy. What are you doing?

Wesley Sticking him in the rubbish, where he belongs.

With JE still bawling through the speaker, Wesley drops it in the waste bin and puts the lid on. JE's muffled voice can be heard shouting in the bin.

Rose You can't do that to your dad, Wesley.

Wesley Exactly, but I can do it to this piece of garbage.

Rose Wesley, where are you going?

Wesley (*walking away*) Out. Anywhere.

Rose (*retrieving speaker*) John, are you alright? Calm down, will you?

JE (*Tannoy*) And don't you start. If it wasn't for you molly-coddling him we wouldn't be in this mess, you and your apron strings, you and your fancy ideas. You're all against me, it's a conspiracy down there, and I won't stand for it any longer, do you understand?

Rose (*dropping Tannoy back in bin and putting lid on*) Oh, go to hell!

SCENE FIVE

Wesley runs into a phone box.

Wesley (*into phone*) Is that the Samaritans? Sarah Stranks, please. No, it's a personal call.

SCENE SIX

Outside the club.

Minutes later. Rose arrives in tears.

Spoon Rose, are you alright?

Rose No, I'm not alright. Oh, Spoon, I don't know which way to turn, I don't know what to do for the best.

Spoon What's happened?

Rose Nothing unusual, nothing that doesn't happen every single day. I don't think I can take it any longer.

Spoon Come here, let me hold you.

Rose You know how I feel, you know who I'd rather be with, but I just feel so guilty.

Spoon You shouldn't feel guilty, Rose, you've devoted you whole life to that man.

Rose I know he's in pain, I know he's hurting, but you can't just love someone out of sympathy, can you? You can't just be with someone because you feel sorry for them.

Spoon Don't cry. You've got me now, Rose, whether you want me or need me or not – I'll always be waiting.

Rose I've tried, I've really tried.

Spoon Come on now, stop crying.

Rose Yes, you're right. I've come here to exercise my democratic right as a woman. Trouble is, who should I vote for? If he loses he'd go to pieces, but if he wins I don't think I could bear being in the same country, let alone in that house.

Spoon In which case . . . Look, just go in there and do what you think's right, Rose.

Rose Do you have a coin?

Spoon A coin – what for?

Rose (*spins coin*) Heads or tails.

Spoon Heads or hearts, more like.

*Rose sighs and goes into the club. Spoon lights up a
cigarette and waits on the doorstep of the club.*

SCENE SEVEN

*Wesley and Sarah in the Pearl of India. Wesley is getting
drunk.*

Sarah Slow down, you're going to drown.

Wesley Drowning your sorrows – that's what they call it,
don't they?

Sarah You don't usually drink, though, do you?

Wesley No, but I think I could get a taste for it. (*Shouts.*)
Another bottle of this Liebfrau . . . milk. Please. Thank
you. Good wine this stuff, without a cork. Saves a lot of
messing around.

Sarah Well if you want my advice, you'll sleep on it.

Wesley Sleep on it? Sleep on it? My dad just called me
queer.

Sarah Or you could sleep with me.

Wesley A queer! Just because I can read. Just because I'm
not some big hairy-arse fireman with a hose instead of a
dick.

Sarah Or you could sleep with me.

Wesley He thinks I'm queer. Well, so what if I was?
Which I'm not by the way.

Sarah Well, if you slept with me . . .

Wesley And he's not even my dad, probably – so what's
it got to do with him anyway?

Sarah If we slept together, wouldn't that prove . . .?

Wesley I've a good mind to take a girl home and sleep with her just to prove it to him once and for all. Sleep with a girl right under his nose. Or a woman, even. Imagine that. Ha!

Sarah Ha!

Wesley But that would be childish, right?

Sarah Right.

Wesley Down on his level.

Sarah Exactly.

Wesley Exactly. Exactly. And I'm better than that.

Sarah Yes, you are. Look, Wes, why don't you let things cool? We could go away for the weekend. Talk things through – you could use me as a . . . sounding board. What about Scotland? You could do a bit of fishing.

Wesley (*draining the bottle*) You're right. No time like the present. Grab the bull by the horns, strike while the iron's hot. That's what you mean, isn't it?

Sarah Precisely. Spot on. Perfect. I think.

Wesley (*standing up*) Thanks, Sarah. You're brilliant. Right, I'm off.

Sarah Off where?

Wesley To fight fire with fire!

SCENE EIGHT

Rose comes back out of the club after voting.

Spoon There, that didn't hurt, did it?

Rose No. One little cross. (*Pecks him on the cheek.*) Goodnight, Spoon.

Spoon Goodnight, Rose.

Rose walks away up the road

Right, let's see how the land's lying.

Spoon goes into the club

Noreen, good turnout?

Noreen Nearly a hundred per cent. Started this morning at nine o'clock on the dot, Mr Castle with his telephone vote, and it hasn't stopped since.

Spoon So who's left?

Noreen Well, going off this list, just two more. Yourself, and Wesley.

Spoon Any indications as to which way it's going?

Noreen Mr Spoon, you'll get me shot. Actually, I've been keeping a running total, and as it stands, it's level-pegging.

Spoon Really? A dead heat?

Noreen Neck and neck. Even-Stephen.

Spoon And only me and Wesley Castle to vote.

Noreen That's the lie of the land.

Spoon Thank you, Noreen, you're a treasure. I'll just go outside and finish this cigarette.

Spoon goes back out onto the doorstep

Wesley (*appearing from the shadows*) Evening.

Spoon Wesley, how long have you been stood there?

Wesley Long enough.

Spoon Is anything the matter?

Wesley On no, I'm the son and heir of the great John Edward Castle, aren't I? What could possibly be wrong?

Spoon Have you been drinking, Wesley?

Wesley I might have had one or two. Sacked from the fire service and thrown out of the house – I'm celebrating! Anyway, what if I am drunk, are you going to offer me a bit of fatherly advice?

Spoon Yes. Do your shoelaces up before you fall over.

Wesley We've a lot in common, me and you, don't you think, Spoon?

Spoon Such as?

Wesley You tell me. Don't you think I've worked it out for myself?

Spoon Look, Wesley, if it's your mother . . .

Wesley Yeah, I'd say she came into it, not to mention mi father. Ironic, wouldn't you say? Me going in there to cast mi lot, to choose between the two of you.

Spoon Well, I don't know if irony's the right word . . .

Wesley I was going to be loyal and sympathetic and all that crap. I was going to do the honourable thing. But after all the stuff he came out with tonight, it's payback time.

Spoon Don't be too hard on him. It can't be easy in his condition – being a father.

Wesley Oh, and what are the perfect conditions for fatherhood, in your experience?

Spoon Yes, you've got a point there. What would I know?

Wesley Oh, I'm sure if you imagine hard enough . . .

Spoon No, not me. Medical problem. Firing blanks.

Never could and never will. No point imagining when it's like that.

Wesley (*dumbstruck*) You mean . . . you mean . . .

Spoon I don't know why I'm telling you all this.

Wesley (*bewildered and crestfallen*) No. Right.

Spoon The policeman that fired blanks. Not surprising I never made the firearms division.

Wesley So I'm back where I started, then.

Spoon And where's that?

Wesley Up the birth canal without a paddle.

Spoon Eh? You're not going to start on about Freud again, are you?

Wesley Well, fuck him. I'm going into that polling booth to give him a taste of his own medicine.

Spoon Sorry, Wesley. It's too late. Voting finished ten minutes ago, look. (*Shows him his watch.*)

Wesley It isn't my day is it? Right, that does it.

Spoon Where are you going?

Wesley Up. I'm going up.

Spoon Up where, up north?

Wesley Yeah, and a bit higher as well.

Spoon goes back into the club.

Spoon Still time, Noreen?

Noreen Yes, one more minute.

Spoon Oh good. My watch must be running a little fast. By the way, I've just spoken to Wesley Castle, seems like he's going to abstain.

Noreen Looks like you've got the deciding vote, then. Fancy that.

Spoon Aye, fancy that.

Gert Castle's bedroom.

Morning. Gert Castle in bed. Phone rings.

Gert Who is it? Ah Noreen, do you have the result? Alright, be like that, you stuck-up – Anyway, how do you know he's here?

Wagstaff (*his head pops out from the foot of the bed*) Who is it?

Gert Noreen Knowles. Wishes to speak with 'outgoing Entertainments Secretary Wagstaff'.

Wagstaff Ah, hello, Wagstaff here, of Wagstaff's Televisual Emporium, for all your viewing requirements at competitive prices. Ah, Noreen, yes I'd just popped in here for a quick . . . er . . . chinwag. Do you have the result? I see, I see. Very good, I'll tell him immediately.

Gert Well?

JE's bedroom.

JE (*picking up phone*) John Edward Castle.

Wagstaff (*on other end of phone*) John Edward, it's Alwin here, with the result.

JE Go on.

Wagstaff (*phone*) Well, John, I have to tell you it was very very close, very close indeed. In fact there was only one vote in it.

JE God damn it. That slimy rat, that greasy toad, worming his way in. I'll kill him, that . . . cocksucker . . . do you hear me, I'll kill him.

Wagstaff (*phone*) Well, if I were you I wouldn't. You might be able to do this job from your bedroom but you'd be struggling from a prison cell in Armley.

JE What? What do you mean?

Wagstaff You won, you great clot. By one vote. By Christ, I thought it might be close but I never thought it would be that close. Anyway, congratulations, John Edward, and let me take this opportunity to wish you all the very best – I've no doubt that you're the right man for the job. John Edward? John?

JE (*croaky tearful whisper*) I won. I won.

SCENE ELEVEN

Narrator
> Meanwhile,
> from the chimney pot of the corner shop,
> white smoke rises up and up,
> as Mr Boot and Mrs Boot
> proclaim John Edward Castle . . . Pope.

Mrs Boot (*burning an election poster of Spoon in the hearth*) More paraffin and a damp rag, in honour of you-know-who?

Mr Boot Don't mind if I do.

Through sound of radio dial trawling across frequencies, fade across to JE.

JE's bedroom.

JE (*radio*) Testing, testing, one, two, three, this is Radio Castle, the voice of Jerusalem. Friends and family, fellow people, citizens of this good town, you tune in at an historic moment in time, you tune in to hear history as it happens. Twenty-five years ago yesterday a man waded into a sea of flames, into the very fires of hell. He paid a heavy price: crushed by falling timbers and scarred by the savage heat, he survived, but what awaited him was only half a life. Lesser men would have mouldered, rotted away, gone to pot, but not this one. This one was made of stronger stuff.

Narrator
       Meanwhile,
       in the back of Number 27
       a bonfire burns in a terrace garden –
       it's Spoon's old van full of clothes and jumble.
       Plumes of smoke ascend to heaven.
       Bleepers go off in the homes of firemen
       but behind the doors of Jerusalem station
       there's an empty space instead of an engine.

Fire station.

Fireman Er, what's the procedure when someone's nicked off with the pump, Sarge?

Sergeant Down to the Hare and Hounds, five pints of lager each, aim for the hottest part of the fire and try not to get your pubes singed, I suppose.

JE's bedroom.

JE (*radio*) People of Jerusalem, John Edward Castle is risen from the ashes, born again from the embers of smouldering hopes and flickering dreams, burning bright with ambition, courage and force. (*Turns radio aside for a moment.*) Only call me for a missing budgie, would you? Only phone me when the poodle went walkabouts? Only need me when the donkey did a runner? Well, there's a new pecking order around this town from now on. (*into mic*) Mother, release the animals!

All the animals file out of Gert's back door.

Narrator
> Ah, the doors of the ark are opened wide
> and out come the animals two by two,
> the elephant and the kangaroo,
> the budgerigar and the cockatoo,
> the poodle, the peacock, the twite and the trout,
> But for every pig there's a snout . . .

The Narrator/Census Taker passes amongst the people of Jerusalem, handing out wads of money.

Zak (*pocketing money*) Not me, man, I don't talk to cops, they're too quick to give a dog a bad name, eh babe?

Jade (*pocketing money*) Yeah. Filth.

Narrator
> And for every crime there's a blabbermouth,
> Someone to cough it up or spill the beans.

Jalopy Joe (*pocketing money*) You wouldn't believe what I find down the back seat of a secondhand motor. What I say is this: when you see the world through a windscreen, you get the full picture.

Cecil (*pocketing money*) I'm a photographic artist. I'd never dream of prying into the nooks and crannies of

71

other people's lives. Now, Kylie, just a little lower, darling, and a little wider.

Narrator
> A squealer, a rat,
> a dobber, a grass,
> Some canary who'll sing . . .

Sugget 1 (*pocketing money*) What goes on between a man and his tailor . . .

Sugget 2 (*pocketing money*) . . . is between him and a tape measure and goes no further.

Twistle (*pocketing money*) The tobacconist is a true gentleman, not one for gossip and tittle-tattle. Whatever I glean goes up in smoke, into the ether.

Narrator
> For every missing poodle or carp
> there's a snitch or a nark
> who'll blow the whistle for twenty quid.

Beardsley 1 (*pocketing money*) It's amazing what you can hear coming up out of a chimney, ain't that right, brother?

Beardsley 2 (*pocketing money*) Yeah, even if it does go in one ear and out the other.

Boysie (*pocketing money*) I can see it all in a customer's eyes. It's working with naked flesh, you see, and cold blood, and sharp knives. That's how it is for a butcher – it's in his nature.

Gert's front door.

Narrator
> And for every snout there's a pig.
> Some rozzer, some copper, some filth, some fuzz,
> laying the law down and locking the cuffs . . .

The Census Taker puts on a policeman's hat.

Census Taker Gert Castle, you are charged with the unlawful taking of three dogs, six cats, four goldfish and numerous other livestock and pets. You have the right to remain silent, but anything you do say will be written down and could be used against you in evidence. Do you have any comment at this time?

Gert Yes, you can . . .

A tidal wave of abuse is drowned out by a braying donkey.

Census Taker Take her away.

Narrator
Meanwhile
reports come in from a Scottish loch
of a vehicle, painted fire-brigade red
and a turntable ladder at total extent,
reaching over the water, fifty yards out,
and a fisherman fishing, perched on the end,
hauling in salmon and hauling in trout.

Scottish loch.

Wesley True peace. The biggest fish in the deepest, calmest water. (*He reels in another fish.*) Come here, my beauty.

Sarah (*from the shore*) Wesley, come and have some breakfast. I've got a fire going. Bring those in and I'll fry them up.

Wesley Are you my good Samaritan, or what?

Sarah I'd cross over to your side of the road anytime, Wesley Castle. Come and have some breakfast. Then . . .

why don't you show me the inside of the cabin again, let me press some more of those buttons, eh?

Wesley I'm on my way right now. Ohhhh – (*Falls into the water.*)

JE's bedroom.

JE (*radio*) Yesterday was a golden day, listeners, a day when the ordinary people of this parish put a cross next to a name, a name that stands for tradition, respect and pride. It was a vote those people will never regret, not as long as they live, not as long as John Edward Castle is Entertainments Secretary of Jerusalem Social Club. Never doubt the determination of a man who's gone it alone for a quarter of a century, a man with an iron will, with steel in his eye and fire in his heart.

Railway station.

Narrator
> Meanwhile,
> at the railway station, nothing moves.
> The hanging baskets drip with dew,
> then onto the platform walks a man –

Spoon arrives on the platform.

Narrator
> with a hat on his head and bags in his hands.
> And a jackdaw lands on the overhead wire.

JE's bedroom.

JE (*radio*) So much for the victor. As for the defeated and demoralised Mr Spoon, I ask him this. How could he show his face now, how could he walk the streets of this town, knowing he tried to step into the shoes of a man crippled and crushed by fate? The people have turned their backs, voted with their feet. Shame on you, Spoon. There's no place for you in Jerusalem. Sneak off into the night like you did all those many moons ago, with your tail between your legs and your head hung low. (*Puts on 'Jerusalem' in background.*)

Railway station.

Narrator
 Then a woman appears from out of the air –

Rose walks onto the platform.

 and doesn't smile or speak, but stands
 with a travelling case, and stares and stares.

 If they both reached out they could almost touch.
 The bird in the tree is a collared dove.
 There's a buzz in the rail and the signals change,
 and the blur of a train divides the town,
 and slows, and stops, and a whistle is blown,
 and when it departs, both birds have flown.
 At vanishing point, you think you can sense
 the coming together of parallel lines.

JE Listeners, let's start as we mean to go on. (*aside*) Rose, get me that cuppa, I'm gagging. (*back on mic*) So, eyes down for your first bingo of the new era – two pounds for a line, five pounds for a full house, and a jackpot of ten quid. Ten quid, ladies and gentlemen – this is a new age, a new dawn. (*Clears his throat.*) On its own, number one . . .

Narrator
 And the tide rises, and the tide falls.

The End.